Ideals
and
Ideologies

Communism,
Socialism,
and
Capitalism

Books by Harry B. Ellis

IDEALS AND IDEOLOGIES:
Communism, Socialism, and Capitalism

THE COMMON MARKET

THE ARABS
(Major Cultures of the World book)

Harry B. Ellis

Ideals and Ideologies

**Communism,
Socialism,
and
Capitalism**

The World Publishing Company
Cleveland and New York

Frontispiece
Left: (Top) A Head Start class in New York City's Harlem; (Bottom) View of Essen in West Germany's booming industrial Ruhr. Right: (Top) Worker in a cabbage field in Russia—new farming techniques are being introduced throughout the Soviet Union; (Center) American and East German soldiers confront one another on August 13, 1961, when Berlin Wall was erected; (Bottom) new style housing in Oliwa, Poland, is typical of postwar construction in many European cities on both sides of the Iron Curtain.

To Ann

Published by The World Publishing Company
2231 West 110th Street, Cleveland, Ohio 44102
Published simultaneously in Canada by
Nelson, Foster & Scott Ltd.
Library of Congress catalog card number: 68-14697
Text copyright © 1968 by Harry B. Ellis
All rights reserved. No part of this book may be reproduced
in any form without written permission from the publisher, except for
brief passages included in a review appearing in a newspaper
or magazine. Printed in the United States of America.
Designed by Audrey Scharff.

Photo Acknowledgments

The author and The World Publishing Company herewith thank the following individuals and institutions whose co-operation has made possible the preparation of *Ideals and Ideologies: Communism, Socialism, and Capitalism.* All possible care has been taken to trace the ownership of every picture included and to make full acknowledgment for its use. If any errors have accidentally occurred, they will be corrected in subsequent editions, provided notification is sent to the publisher.

AFL-CIO News, for illustrations on pp. 205, 219

APN-Foto, for illustrations on frontispiece (top right) and pp. 66, 81

The Arab Information Center, for illustration on p. 114

Aufnahme der Landesbildstelle Berlin, for illustrations on frontispiece (center right) pp. 47, 48, 49, 50, 55, 57, 59, 108, 109, 111, 122, 175, and 179

The Bettmann Archive, Inc., for illustration on p. 137

The British Information Services, for illustrations on pp. 161, 162, 166, 167, and 240

CAF, for illustrations on frontispiece (bottom right) and pp. 13, 15, 17, 61, 80, and 120

73785

The Christian Science Monitor, for illustrations on pp. 68 and 69

Paul Conklin, for illustrations on pp. 223 and 227

The Consolidated Edison Company of New York, Inc., for illustrations on pp. 234 and 235

George Eastman House, for illustration on p. 211

James Foote, for illustrations on pp. 194 and 195

Fotoreporter, for illustration on p. 87

Israel Information Service, for illustrations on pp. 132 and 133

Kaiser Steel Corporation, for illustration on p. 201

MTI Foto-Sziklai Dezsó felv, for illustration on p. 18

Office of Education, for illustration on frontispiece (top left)

Presseabteilung der Botschaft der UdSSR, for illustration on p. 21

Presse und Informationsamt der Bundesregierung, for illustrations on frontispiece (bottom left) and pp. 60, 98, 116, 144, 145, 173, 174, 175 and 179

The Radio Times Hulton Picture Library, for illustrations on p. 164

Standard Oil Company, for illustrations on pp. 186 and 187

The Swedish International Press Bureau, for illustrations on pp. 22, 107, 149, 150, 151, 155, 158, 237, and 239

United Nations, for illustrations on pp. 41, 44, 65, 75, and 101

Wide World Photos, for illustrations on pp. 26, 30, 33, 37, 42, 94, 95, 184, 215, 220, 221, and 229

Contents

ACKNOWLEDGMENTS

The author wishes to express his thanks to many officials and private citizens of the United States, Britain, France, West Germany, East Germany, Sweden, Poland, Czechoslovakia, and other countries, who so kindly shared their time and knowledge during the writing of this book. He is particularly grateful to James Brown and Harry Trend of Radio Free Europe, and to Vidkunn Ulriksson of the American Embassy in Bonn, for their special help.

Marx and
Dr. Kildare

THE MANAGER of the European factory was short and powerfully built, a former worker himself by the looks. His eyes sparkled as he outlined the operation of his plant. "We make two types of railroad cranes," he explained, "a large one and a small one. Our small crane"—he beamed with pride—"now has a rating of Q."

"What does that mean?" I asked.

"Highest quality," he replied. "The government's Plan Organization assigns a quality rating to everything manufactured in this country. Highest rating is Q. Then comes rating Number One and others below that.

"Periodically inspectors from the government's quality-control unit come to look us over. If our small crane measures up to Q, we get two per cent more from the government for each machine. This is divided among the workers as I see fit, the most going to those people who do the best job.

"If, on the other hand," he continued, "our cranes don't measure up to their assigned Q, the government takes five per cent off the price."

"Isn't that the profit motive?" I asked.

The manager hesitated. Clearly he preferred to use other words. "Through this system," he rejoined, "a worker has a stake in his job. The more efficient he is, the more money he gets."

The man to whom I spoke was a Communist, sporting a party membership badge in his lapel. His was no private enterprise plant. He directed a People's Own Factory in the city of Leipzig, in Communist East Germany. To improve the quality of its output, to compete on the world market, this state-owned factory had come around to using a "capitalist" device—the profit motive.

In a different part of East Germany I visited another Communist enterprise, a collective farm directed by a huge, friendly young man. He was a dentist's son, but his bulk and great work-roughened hands made him look like what he was—a farmer. He had chosen to work on a farm and now he was chairman of an East German collective near the Polish border.

The farm he directed comprised 1,450 acres. Its soil was sandy and he made no great claims for it. Soil in other parts of the country was better, he maintained. Some 113 members belonged to his collective, which had been started in 1954 when a number of small farmers had pooled their land, animals, and equipment in one large unit. The new farm was named LPG (Agricultural Production Society, or collective) Pascha Angelina Manschnow.

A picture of the original owner of that melodic name

hung on the wall of the chairman's office. She had been a Russian woman, important in Soviet agriculture, but in what way the German did not know. He was a relative newcomer to the farm, he explained.

He had been studying scientific farming at Humboldt University in East Berlin when he had received a call to LPG Manschnow. It appeared that the former chairman, a faithful Communist, had not gotten along well with the members of the collective, so they had voted him out. The young giant with the farmer's hands and a dentist father was his successor.

"Are you also a member of the party?" I asked. The young man smiled. After his election, he had joined. It made good sense, for he had to work through the government to run his farm.

Despite his newness to the party, the director was enthusiastic about collective farming. Until 1960, when the government had put on pressure to collectivize, most East German farms had been privately owned. Now more than 90 per cent of the nation's farmland was grouped in collectives.

In most such state-controlled farms, like LPG Manschnow, the farmer retained title to his land but sold his animals and equipment to the collective. When the year's income was divided up, the director explained, each member family received between four and five thousand marks, or about one thousand dollars. Each family also was given feed grains and potatoes, plus about six dollars for each hectare (2.471 acres) of land he had brought into the LPG.

There was another source of income. Each family farmed privately about one acre of land. This was a large truck garden, in which the farmer grew his own choice of vegetables. The collective, on the other hand, concentrated on a few main crops—wheat, barley, potatoes, fodder, or sugar beets—whatever was suited to soil and climate. What a man raised on his private plot he could sell on the open market. If he kept no animals on his acre of land, he received 630 marks yearly in lieu of feed grains.

"Can a farmer take his land out of the collective?" I inquired.

"Theoretically, yes," was the answer. "But no one has done so. If he did, he would have to take a piece of land somewhere on the edge, so as not to disrupt the farming."

The young director had left much unsaid. A farmer who quit LPG Manschnow, or any other East German collective, would be cut off from government sources of credit, fertilizer, and seed. He could not afford to buy new animals and machinery, even if he could find them. Government channels for marketing his crops would be closed. That is why, though the director did not say so, 90 per cent of East German farmers had joined collectives in the first place.

Recently I drove through many miles of farmland in western Poland, not far from LPG Manschnow. Poland also is a Communist country. Stout Polish peasants bending over their crops looked very much like their East German counterparts. But there was a fundamental difference. The Poles were working their own farms.

Like other Communist regimes, that of Poland also had collectivized. At one time the government controlled 75 per cent of Polish land. Now the same government is turning back land to private farmers just as fast as it can. What is more, the Polish Government helps private farmers by making credit, mechanized equipment, and

Ammoniated water is poured on the fields of a Polish state farm. Poland is one of the first countries in Europe to use ammoniated water in agriculture.

marketing aids available through the medium of village agricultural circles, or co-operatives. Why?

"Collectives did not work in Poland," bluntly replied a Communist official in Warsaw. "The Polish peasant is a stubborn man, attached to his own land. Collectives simply lowered his incentive to be efficient—without increasing production."

So Communist Poland tore up Marxist rules and broke up the collectives. The East German Government works hard to collectivize all the land in the country. The Warsaw regime works just as hard to give it all back to the farmers.

What does this mean? Simply that the textbook of Karl

Marx no longer means the same thing everywhere in the Communist world. Governments adapt the rules to fit their people's needs—all the while insisting they are as Communist as ever.

In a certain European country live several people who sign checks for whatever they want to buy—furniture, fur coats, a new car, or even a weekend house in the country. Stores and banks forward their checks to the government, which pays the bills. Are these people members of a royal family? No, they are East German scientists, professors, inventors—men whose contributions to the state are so vital that a grateful Communist regime gives them whatever they want.

Holders of these "personal accounts," as they are called, are a favored few. But an East German intellectual farther down the ladder talked about a government resort in the Harz Mountains, near Czechoslovakia, which he and his wife were entitled to visit. They were not members of the Communist Party. But as an engineer whose skill was useful to the state, this citizen could visit vacation spots closed to ordinary folk.

The Harz Mountain hotel, he confided, was the last word in luxury. A double room with bath, plus all meals, cost his wife and himself $14 per day. "The last time we were there," the engineer added, "we saw only one guest wearing a party pin. People avoided him."

Do average East Germans—the proletariat in whose name communism triumphed—know about the Harz resort? Not if their government can help it.

On Warsaw's busy shopping street called Nowy Swiat, I gazed through the window of a large radio and TV store. Most prices on the sets inside were marked in Polish

A busy shopping intersection in modern Warsaw

zlotys. But the price tags on two TV sets standing on a separate table were quoted in dollars—$123 and $128. The sets were Polish, and so were potential customers in the store. The riddle of why the sets were priced in dollars was explained by a Warsaw economist.

"Poles today," he said, "are allowed to accumulate foreign currency. But they cannot spend it in private trade. They must deal through PKO, or the Polish Assistance Bank.

"If a Polish-American, for example, wants to give dollars to a cousin in Poland, he sends the money to the PKO. The latter opens a drawing account for the lucky man. Let's say the cousin wants a new TV. He goes to the store, picks out one of the sets marked in dollars, and orders it. PKO simply debits his account for that amount.

"The Pole with a cousin in Chicago or Hamtramck has his new TV. The state gets some foreign exchange."

Before World War II the Soviet Union was the only communist nation in the World. After the war the Soviets imposed communism in Europe wherever the Red Army had conquered in the war against the Germans. The Iron Curtain clanged down as an unbroken slash of barbed wire 860 miles long, from Lübeck on the Baltic Sea to the German-Czechoslovakian border. Germany was cut in two. East of this bristling frontier communism rules, planted and nourished by Soviet power. West of the Iron Curtain lies the free world, shielded by the United States.

Neither America nor the Soviet Union treads on the other's toes. Behind this tough political façade, however, ways of governing are changing. Western regimes, including the United States government, use concepts originally called socialist to meet the needs of poor, sick, and aged citizens. We call these programs social security.

Communist governments east of the Iron Curtain also have adapted. They can keep their people from escaping physically to the West. But they cannot keep the influence of Western books, films, and television programs from seeping through the Iron Curtain.

Recently, for example, several schools in a large Polish city asked their pupils to name their favorite hero. The earnest Marxists who thought up this question must have wished they hadn't. Tops with Polish youngsters, it turned out, was "Dr. Kildare." Second came "The Saint."

Every Polish child who had the chance watched these characters on TV, in films rented by their government's

Polish students in the reading room of a city public library

television network. Nor was it only youngsters who watched. "The Communist Party," drawled a Polish journalist in Warsaw, "knows better than to schedule a meeting during Dr. Kildare's TV show. No one would come."

Following Dr. Kildare on Polish TV screens was a French-language course called "French in Your Home." Even more popular were Walter and Connie, an English couple who taught English by TV, via the British Broadcasting Corporation.

"Until 1956," reported a Polish intellectual, "all Polish children had to study Russian in school. Now they can choose. First choice is English, followed by German." At the bottom of the list, according to this Pole, came Russian.

Western ideas breed knowledge. Organizations like Radio Free Europe, Voice of America, and Radio Liberty pump information about the free world behind the Iron Curtain. Workers in Communist factories know their take-home pay cannot compare with that of workers in the United States, or Holland, or Luxembourg. What they may not yet know is that social security systems in the West are just as generous as those in the Soviet bloc, and often more so.

Workers behind the Iron Curtain, however, have learned enough about conditions in the West to put pressure on their leaders for a better standard of living. Revolt broke out twice behind the Iron Curtain—in East Germany in 1953, in Hungary in 1956. Both times Soviet troops and tanks restored order. In 1968 the Red Army invaded Czechoslovakia to curb a liberalization movement. Despite these Soviet interventions, civilian pressures continued. To ease them Communist rulers promised less police rule, more

A view of new housing in modern Budapest, Hungary. By putting pressures on Communist rulers, many workers behind the Iron Curtain now enjoy a high standard of living.

In the last twenty years, Hungarian motorcycles have become popular all over Europe.

consumer goods. Intent on building up heavy industry, Communist regimes in the past had paid too little attention to the quality of things people needed to wear and use in their homes. Warehouses were choked with shoddy goods which people would not buy. Influenced by the West, women in Prague, Budapest, and Cracow demanded better styling. The new fashions hopped the Iron Curtain and appeared on Warsaw streets almost as soon as they hit Paris and Stockholm.

But how could workers under communism be persuaded to turn out more and better shoes, suits, radios, frying pans? By giving them rewards. The profit motive, as in the People's Own Factory at Leipzig, mushroomed throughout Eastern Europe. In 1965 Soviet Premier Aleksei N. Kosygin sanctioned bonuses and other rewards for workers in Soviet industry. By 1970, Mr. Kosygin pledged, the entire Soviet economy would be profit-oriented.

One of the first Soviet plants to introduce the new system, according to the *New York Times*, was the First

A state-owned dairy farm in Russia

Moscow Watch Factory, which turned out two million men's watches yearly. Under the incentive system, officials told visitors, the factory was allowed to keep 18 per cent of its profits to reward workers and improve their working conditions. Production losses through careless handling of watches had dropped 29 per cent since introduction of the plan.

The new system developed so well that a leading Soviet economist updated Mr. Kosygin's prediction. By the end of 1968, this economist said, all Soviet factories would be "reformed." During 1966, he added, plants operating on an incentive basis had run up profits of 25 per cent, compared with 10 per cent for the Soviet economy as a whole.

Communism is not the only political movement making hash of the old shibboleths of ideology. Sweden has been governed by the Social Democratic Party since 1932. The social welfare program fashioned by this government be-

20

came a model for many countries in the world. When a Westerner today speaks of socialism in practice, he tends to think of Sweden.

But 90 per cent of the Swedish economy is privately owned. Almost all Swedes work for private firms. What little the government does own was mostly nationalized before the Social Democrats came to power, like iron mines in the frozen north, whose survival depended on government subsidy. Sweden, in fact, is a private enterprise land.

France calls itself a capitalist country. Most French businessmen distrust socialism. But the nation's largest employer is the French Government, which hires millions of workers in state-owned railroads, radio and television networks, gas and electric works, the Renault car company, even some banks and insurance companies. Capitalist France has much less free enterprise than Socialist Sweden.

21

A mining town in the north of Sweden, where open-cut mining has now been replaced by underground operations

For several years my family and I lived in a small European town. Every month, like clockwork, a man on a motorbike stopped at a house near ours and handed the lady of the house the equivalent of $55. The woman in the next house got only $8 from his leather pouch. But the housewife in the place on the corner, whose yard was filled with bicycles, toys, and a rabbit hutch, received the whopping sum of $120 from the man on the motorbike.

There was nothing unique about our town. The same thing happened every month of every year in every city, town, and village throughout the nation. The women who received this largess had done nothing to earn the money —except become mothers. These family allowances were one aspect of an all-pervasive social security system, protecting every citizen from birth to death.

Surely this was a Communist land, or at least Socialist? Not at all. This was capitalist France.

What we are experiencing in today's world, as the above examples show, is a crumbling of ideology in the business community. Most of the world's four billion people live under systems called communist, socialist, or capitalist. Their governments cling to these political labels. More and more, however, these same communist, socialist, and capitalist governments use similar techniques to manage their economies.

President Lyndon B. Johnson acknowledged this in December 1966 when he asked McGeorge Bundy, president of the Ford Foundation, to undertake a special mission. Mr. Bundy was to explore the possibility of setting up a permanent organization, through which the United States, the Soviet Union, and other advanced nations could share management techniques. In such a forum Communists and capitalists would leave party labels outside the door, roll up their sleeves, and discuss how to solve industrial problems common to both. Mr. Bundy told reporters the forum they had in mind might be called International Center for Studies of Common Problems of Advanced Societies.

Ideology is defined as a system of theories and aims which gives intellectual inspiration to a culture or to a political movement. Thus we distinguish between differing types of political and economic theory by calling them communist ideology, socialist ideology, capitalist ideology, and so on.

In a lecture he gave in Germany in late 1966 Dr. John Kenneth Galbraith, Harvard economist and former American Ambassador to India, posed the following question.

What role does ideology play in economic management today? Governments, he pointed out, which had achieved economic success had widely differing ideological approaches. They tried to explain their prosperity in different ways.

"West Germans," he declared, "say their success has come through a free-market economy. Norwegians claim their equal success has come through planned socialism."

The conclusion, according to Dr. Galbraith, was that ideological explanations fell apart. "Conservatives," he said, "attribute economic success to substantial resistance to socialism." Liberals claimed just the opposite—that success was due to the tempering of capitalism to meet people's welfare needs. "We should be painfully suspicious," Dr. Galbraith maintained, "of loose ideological categories and of people who explain matters in this way." Our task in this book is to dust off the words communism, socialism, and capitalism, which for so long have been stereotyped, and examine their status in today's world. In the process we may learn surprising things, for the world —on both sides of the Iron Curtain—has moved a long way since Bolsheviks first raised the Red flag of revolution in Russia in 1917.

From Marx
to Stalin

COMMUNISM as a communal sharing of property is older than Jesus and his disciples, as modern as kibbutzim in the state of Israel. But the political movement which we call communism derived from Karl Marx, a nineteenth-century German philosopher. To Marx, the history of mankind was a story of class struggle.

"Freeman and slave," he wrote in *The Communist Manifesto*, "patrician and plebian, lord and serf . . . in a word, oppressor and oppressed, stood in constant opposition to one another, carried on an uninterrupted, now hidden, now open fight, a fight that each time ended, either in a revolutionary reconstitution of society at large, or in the common ruin of the contending classes."

By his own time, Marx wrote, the historic clash had narrowed down to a confrontation between two hostile classes—bourgeoisie and proletariat. By proletariat Marx

25

View of Karl Marx statue, in Moscow. To Marx, the father of communism, the history of mankind was a story of class struggle.

meant the working class, toiling for property owners, or bourgeoisie. The worker had neither property nor political rights. "The executive of the modern State," Marx asserted, "is but a committee for managing the common affairs of the whole bourgeoisie."

In the scramble of the bourgeoisie for markets, small capitalists were squeezed out and power tended to concentrate in the hands of giant industrial firms. Competing against one another, these giants could sell only by lowering the prices of their goods. Wages, as a major item of cost in producing goods, were reduced to the minimum that a man needed to keep himself alive.

Marxist theory held that this exploited worker, and he alone, created all the value of the goods sold by the capitalist. Yet the worker by no means received wages equal to the full value of the things he made. "Surplus value"— the difference between the laborer's wage and the sale price of the item—went to the capitalist. He became rich by sucking up the "surplus value" of the goods manufactured by his workers.

These profits the capitalist invested in machines, which were more efficient than men's hands. New markets must be found to absorb this soaring production. Ships and soldiers of empire-building nations—England, France, Holland, and others—became the tools by which capitalists carved out fresh markets. Colonies overseas furnished raw materials for the churning factories of Europe and at the same time opened new markets to which finished products could be sent.

Machines, turning out more and better goods more cheaply, became the key to competitive success. But machines displaced workers. "The spinning-wheel, the hand-loom," wrote Friedrich Engels, co-author with Marx of *The Communist Manifesto,* "the blacksmith's hammer were replaced by the spinning-machine, the power-loom, the steam-hammer; the individual workshop, by the factory involving the cooperation of hundreds and thousands of workmen." The worker had lost his sense of identity with the goods he made. Now, as machines took his place, the worker lost his job.

This created unemployment, or, as Engels called it, an "industrial reserve army," used by capitalists to keep wages low. If workers in a factory complained of their low pay, there were always others eager to take their place. But workers without jobs could not buy. Home markets dried up. The market place became glutted with goods that could not be sold. The inevitable result was depression, or economic crash.

The laws of capitalist production, in the Marxist view, had brought about these crashes every ten years, beginning with 1825, when industrialization was replacing the old feudal organization of society in much of Western Europe. From such periodic crises, Marx and Engels reasoned, revolution was the only escape. Dispossessed workers must rise up and wrest the means of production from capitalist hands.

"The weapons with which the bourgeoisie brought feudalism to the ground," thundered *The Communist Manifesto* of 1848, "are now turned against the bourgeoisie itself . . . not only has the bourgeoisie forged the weapons that bring death to itself; it has also called into existence the men who are to wield those weapons—the modern working class—the proletariat."

Communists had no lesser goal than the "forcible overthrow of all existing social conditions. Let the ruling classes tremble at a Communistic revolution," concluded the *Manifesto*. "The proletarians have nothing to lose but their chains. They have a world to win."

"WORKINGMEN OF ALL COUNTRIES, UNITE!" For more than a century this final sentence of *The Communist Manifesto* has echoed throughout the world. It still does. Each morning in Bonn a daily newspaper called *Neues Deutschland* (New Germany) crossed my desk. At the top of page one of this organ of the Communist Party of East Germany stand the words *"Proletarier aller Länder, vereinigt euch!"*—the original German version of Marx's famous call to revolution. When Marx and Engels wrote those words in 1848, not a single man lived under communism. Today more than a billion do.

The proletariat by itself, Marx and Engels knew, was an impotent giant. Its powers needed guidance to be set free. The Communist Party would be that guide, standing always in the forefront of the toiling masses. Communists would direct the revolution. Then they would govern—first, where the revolution had taken place; finally, the world.

Accomplishment of so vast a task demanded discipline. A Communist must think of himself as a soldier, loyal only to the party. Orders from above were to be obeyed without question, for they came from interpreters of an exact science. Key words in this science were "dialectics" and "materialism."

Dialectics was defined by Marx as the reality of change through the struggle of opposites—i.e., bourgeoisie and proletariat in the nineteenth century. That which changed was the material world, governed by laws operating independently of human or divine will. Over many centuries these laws had changed and rechanged the shape of society, but men never had understood how or why. Now Marx had taken away the veil. The darkness had been lighted for Communists, vanguard of the proletariat, to seize political and economic power, introduce a classless society, and end the age-old struggle of opposites. Society would float serene on a Communist sea, governed by the dictum: "From each according to his ability, to each according to his needs!"

This would be accomplished by stages. Communism would not emerge full-blown as a child of the revolution.

The three heroes of communism, from left, V. I. Lenin, Friedrich Engels, and Karl Marx, are paraded in a huge sign at a May Day celebration in Red Square in Moscow

First step was for the proletariat to seize the means of production—factories, lands, machines. These would be transferred from private to common ownership. The "people" would own the state, which, however, would be administered by the Communist Party. This stage of the Communist revolution was labeled dictatorship of the proletariat.

The state, in Marxist terms, had existed from time immemorial to protect the rich and repress the poor. Now the tables would be turned. The new state, dictatorship of the proletariat, would repress the former bourgeoisie until it disappeared. Then society would be classless. Once this had occurred, the state itself no longer would be needed. It would, according to Engels, "wither away." Communism would have been established.

Marx conceived of Germany as the country most ripe for revolution. The German working class, in his view, was "much more developed" than that of England and France in the eighteenth and early nineteenth centuries, when the industrial revolution was transforming those nations. Germany's industrial revolution, he predicted, would be followed "immediately" by an uprising of the proletariat.

Conversely, Marx excluded the United States, Britain, and the Netherlands from the inevitability of Communist revolution, since democratic institutions already had been established there. This exclusion later was erased by the Russian Communist leader Nikolai Lenin, who interpreted the teachings of Marx as universally applicable.

By definition a Communist revolution demanded an industrialized country as its focus, where a militant and organized proletariat had had a chance to develop. The revolution of 1917, however, exploded in Czarist Russia, one of the most backward lands in Europe.

There were reasons for this. On the one hand the centuries-old regime of the Czars had become intolerably repressive, symbolized by the bloody crushing of a peaceful strike movement in St. Petersburg in January 1905. Workers in the very act of trying to present a petition to their Czar were cut down ruthlessly by the sovereign's sword-wielding Cossacks. Few workers after 1905 maintained faith in the benevolence of their "Little Father" on the throne.

Second, what little industry Russia possessed before World War I was largely controlled by foreign capital. This meant the country's future development lay partly in non-Russian hands. Third, the great inert mass of Russian peasantry—82 per cent of the population—had shown itself indifferent or hostile to change.

For these and other reasons Russian Marxists saw little possibility of helping the working class through the existing regime. But what could they do? Traditional Marxist theory would have had Russia submit to a long chain of events before the country was deemed ready for Communist revolution. Industry would have had to be developed. This in turn would have led, in the Western European pattern, to the gradual rise of a capitalist society, in which bourgeoisie and proletariat would have been pitted against each other. Such unfoldment would have consumed decades of time.

Some Marxists saw no alternative but to wait, guiding Russia along a gradualist path. Others, led by Nikolai Lenin, disagreed. This group was called Bolsheviks, meaning "majority," as opposed to another Marxist faction named Mensheviks, or "minority." But it was neither Bolsheviks nor Mensheviks who launched the first revolution of 1917. This erupted in Petrograd (now Leningrad) in March of that year, a spontaneous outburst of discontent triggered by Russia's huge losses and sufferings in World War I. Czar Nicholas II was overthrown and in his place a provisional government under Aleksandr Kerensky was established.

This regime had no chance to consolidate itself. In November 1917 Lenin led a small group of Bolsheviks in revolt against Kerensky and founded the first Marxist

Aleksandr Kerensky. The former leader, who escaped from Russia in 1918, now lives in the United States.

government in the world. Though his goals were those of Marx, Lenin had no schooled proletariat behind him to carry out a Marxist program. Most Russians were unorganized peasants. They might be used to support a revolution, but could not conduct it. Urban Russian workers were discontented enough, but unskilled as revolutionaries.

Karl Marx, in other words, had developed his revolutionary theory to fit industrialized states. Lenin was the first disciple of Marx to put theory into practice. But he did so in Russia, the largest country in the world, inhabited by a sprawling rural society. How could this Russia be transformed into a modern industrial state, in which communism might be introduced?

Lenin's solution was to vest total power in a tight core of professional revolutionaries, whose directives were to be obeyed without question by the rank and file. Proletariat and peasantry alike would be told what to do. Should they resist, as countless did, police power would be employed to coerce them. Police and army would become tools of the party.

"We do not need any opposition now, comrades," Lenin warned Russian Communists in 1921. "It is no good reproaching me: it follows from the state of affairs. No more opposition now, comrades."

Thus was born what later became a world-wide phenomenon of the Communist movement—the doctrine of infallibility of the policy-making organ of the Communist Party. In most countries this organ is called Politburo (Political Bureau). In the Soviet Union the name Politburo was changed to Presidium in 1952.

Each national Communist Party has its Politburo, whose word is law. This writ extends throughout the party, even in countries where Communists are out of power. As soon as Communists seize control in a country, the Politburo rules the nation, though its membership and that of the government are not synonymous. In most Communist societies, for example, the chief of state and the prime minister of the government are less important figures than the first secretary of the Communist Party, who heads the Politburo, or Presidium.

Lenin perceived that even his monolithic party would have to follow devious routes toward Marxist goals. In 1921 he introduced his New Economic Policy, or NEP.

This allowed peasants to produce and sell their crops freely. Light industry was returned largely to private ownership, to boost the flow of consumer goods onto the market. To buy these goods, peasants sowed more crops. Only heavy industry remained firmly in government hands.

This retreat from orthodoxy was shrewdly conceived to lessen peasant and worker unrest during the party's early shaky days. The New Economic Policy lasted until 1928, when the economic wounds of World War I had been largely healed. Then came a harsh reversion to Marxism—a ruthless drive to collectivize all farms and to concentrate on heavy industry.

Russian Communists felt themselves surrounded by a hostile capitalist world. Lenin's dream of a supporting revolution in Germany had not come true. Only through self-reliance could the new Soviet state protect and develop itself. Key to this was the expansion of heavy industry, a program which had the accompanying aim of making factory workers out of peasants no longer needed on the farms. Throughout this whole process the management of Russia's economy adhered strictly to Lenin's rule of tight control at the top.

Lenin's concept of a monolithic party, and his theories for applying Marxism to an underdeveloped economy, added a new dimension to the "science" of Karl Marx. To Communists throughout the world the movement became known as Marxism-Leninism. These two men remain undisputed stars in the Marxist firmament.

Not surprisingly, Lenin's example was followed wherever communism triumphed in Europe outside the Soviet Union. Except in Yugoslavia, which had its own revolution, East European Communists rode to victory on Red

Army coattails. It was natural for Bulgarian, Romanian, Czech, and East German Communists to copy the master model; in fact, impossible for them to do otherwise. Also, except in Czechoslovakia and East Germany, communism took root in backward agrarian lands which faced, in miniature, the same development problems as the Soviet Union.

Successor to Lenin as Communist Czar of Russia was Joseph V. Dzhugashvili, whose adopted name—Stalin, man of steel—aptly describes his character. Stalin was a product of the centralized party dictatorship which Lenin had created. Moving up through its ranks, eliminating his rivals one by one, Stalin emerged at the top of a party fashioned to his needs. Purge, police terror, forced-labor camps in remote Siberia—these became hallmarks of Stalin's reign.

In the economic field he was equally relentless. Lenin had been forced to temporize with his New Economic Policy. By 1929, when Stalin had consolidated his power five years after Lenin's death, Russia achieved its prewar level of industrialization. Now, through successive Five-Year Plans, Stalin pushed ruthlessly on to expand Russia's heavy industrial base. At the same time he crushed out the kulak, or rich peasant, class and collectivized Soviet farmland.

Millions of peasants died anonymously during Stalin's drive to rivet the countryside to state control. Political rivals within the Communist Party died more spectacularly, following rigged trials featuring bizarre confessions of guilt by men whose only crime was to disagree with Stalin. This compulsion of Communists to confess their guilt is hard for Westerners to understand.

Premier Stalin of Russia, as he appeared at the height of his power in January 1950

It derives from the Communist conviction that Marxism-Leninism is the one true source of human wisdom, from which party policies naturally flow. This conviction enables Communists to obey the dictates of party leaders with faith and trust. Such a Communist, attacked suddenly by his own leaders as a "deviationist" or anti-Socialist being, is left utterly alone. Where can he turn?

His whole life has been wrapped up in service to the

cause. Without that he is nothing. There still is one way, his oppressors suggest to him, for the victim to serve the party—to confess his guilt, though he may have no idea what he has done wrong. Not to confess means to die in outer darkness, a cipher. To confess also means to die, but comforted by the belief that the Communist has made one last contribution to the cause.

In 1962 a book was published in the Soviet Union which shocked countless Russians. Titled *One Day in the Life of Ivan Denisovich*, this short novel, based on the personal experience of the author, detailed a single day spent by a prisoner in the frozen wastes of a Stalinist forced-labor camp in Siberia. An extra bowl of watery fish soup spelled happiness for the wretched Ivan Denisovich that day. So did a cigarette butt mutely begged from a luckier friend.

This Soviet citizen had been convicted of high treason against the state and sent to to Siberia, cut off from family and friends. His "crime" had been, as a Soviet soldier, to have been captured by the German Army in the bitter fighting of World War II. Denisovich had escaped and made his way back to his own lines. There he had told the truth—he had been captured and had escaped. Unable to believe so straightforward a tale, his Communist superiors charged him with spying for the Germans. Otherwise why would he have turned up again inside Russian lines? Such was the poisoned atmosphere of Stalinist Russia.

No nation suffered more from the war than the Soviet Union. Russian losses, civilian and military, mounted to nineteen million killed, plus the deliberate ruin of towns, crops, and livestock by the German Army. Yet World War II had the effect of allowing communism for the first time to expand beyond the borders of the Soviet Union.

Until the Red Army broke out of its own country in pursuit of the Germans, communism in power had been confined to one nation. During the 1920's and after, the Bolsheviks had added vast internal territories to their effective domain. Lenin's original Constitution of 1918 had covered only that part of the country called the Russian Soviet Federated Socialist Republic.

As Communist influence spread, other "republics" were carved out of the old Czarist empire in Central Asia. In 1922 the name of the country was changed to the Union of Soviet Socialist Republics, or USSR. (Soviet is a Russian word meaning "council." The Communist system consisted of a pyramid of village, regional, and republic councils, culminating in the Supreme Soviet of the USSR. In fact political authority resided with the Politburo of the Central Committee of the Communist Party in Moscow.) This amalgamation of new republics, while impressive, simply put under Communist control roughly the same territory over which the Czars had reigned.

The outbreak of war gave Stalin an opportunity to expand his holdings. The process started in 1940, when the Baltic states of Latvia, Estonia, and Lithuania were incorporated into the Soviet Union. Parts of Finland followed. Moldavia was taken from Romania. Eastern Poland and, after the war, the northern part of German East Prussia were annexed. Czechoslovakia lost Ruthenia. All these territories became part of the USSR itself.

The end of hostilities found Soviet troops occupying huge tracts of Eastern and Central Europe. Poland and the Balkan area in particular were characterized by economic distress, political fragmentation, and the age-old rivalries of national groups. Added to this were war weariness and the hardships of occupation by the Nazis.

Uprooted in every sense, the area was ripe for Soviet intervention.

By 1948 local Communist parties, backed by the Soviet Union, had acquired total power in Hungary, Romania, Bulgaria, and Czechoslovakia. The process in these countries had started with postwar coalition governments, in which non-Communist parties also had been represented. Gradually the others were squeezed out, until Communists were in complete control. In Poland the result was the same, but Polish Communists had been openly aided by the Red Army in tracking down and eliminating opposition.

East Germany was a special case. By wartime agreement among the Allies, postwar Germany had been divided into four parts. The Soviets occupied eastern Germany, and the United States, Britain, and France straddled western portions of Hitler's defeated Reich. During the war German Communists had been carefully trained in Russia. These men, under the leadership of Walter Ulbricht and protected by twenty Soviet divisions, were installed by Moscow in East Berlin. In 1949 Mr. Ulbricht's domain emerged as the German Democratic Republic (GDR). It still is occupied by thousands of Russian troops.

Yugoslavia was unique. There a Communist leader named Marshal Tito had fought a two-pronged battle during World War II—against the Nazi invaders and against anti-Communist Yugoslav forces. By the end of the war Tito had mastered his country and Yugoslavia emerged as the only European state, other than the Soviet Union, to have carried through an indigenous Communist revolution. Yugoslav Communists helped Enver Hoxha establish a Communist regime in tiny Albania, Yugoslavia's southern neighbor.

Marshal Tito of Yugoslavia is seated as he waits to address a session of the General Assembly during an official visit to the United Nations.

Of enormous and as yet incalculable import to the world was the conquest of China for communism by Marxists led by Mao Tse-tung. From 1935 to 1947, while Chinese Nationalist forces were being chewed up in war against the Japanese, the Communists shrewdly instituted land reform, lowered food prices, rents, and taxes, and governed efficiently in the small part of China they controlled. Mao, unlike Lenin in Russia, based his revolution on peasant support. By the end of 1949 the Communists had

Red Chinese leader Mao Tse-tung escorts Albanian Premier Mehmet Shehu during a visit to Red China. Albania, a Communist nation, has close ties with Red China.

As part of a student demonstration in Red China, marchers carry banners and a portrait of Mao. The Red Chinese leader has expressed his approval of student involvement in purges.

driven Chiang Kai-shek's Nationalists from the mainland
to the island of Formosa (Taiwan), and Mao was master
of China.

Two other Asian nations suffered a fate similar to Germany's and were divided after the war. Russia occupied
northern Korea and in 1948 established the North Korean
People's Republic. A bitter war from 1950 to 1953 froze
the 38th parallel as a little Iron Curtain between Communist North Korea and the South Korean Republic.

Vietnam's complex emergence from Japanese occupation and French colonial rule resulted in the establishment
of Communist control in North Vietnam, under the leadership of Ho Chi Minh. Vietnam remains one place in the
world where a firm line of demarcation between Communist and non-Communist influence has not been
clearly drawn.

In 1958 a bearded young revolutionary named Fidel
Castro led a 26th of July Movement that toppled the
Batista regime from power in Cuba. Gradually Castro un-
veiled himself as a Communist and Cuba today ranks as the
fourteenth nation to enter the sphere of communism.[1]
Of this total the Soviet Union, Yugoslavia, China, Cuba,
and to some extent North Vietnam, are the only ones to
have carried through their own versions of Marxist revolution. Communists in the remaining nine states owe
their success primarily to Moscow and, in the case of
Albania, to Yugoslavia.

Of the world's three superpowers, two—the Soviet

---

[1] The Soviet Union, Yugoslavia, Albania, Bulgaria, Czechoslovakia,
East Germany, Hungary, Poland, Romania, China, Outer Mongolia,
North Korea, North Vietnam, and Cuba.

Premier Fidel Castro of Cuba during a visit in 1959 to the United Nations

Union and China—are Communist. One-fourth of the world's people, 700,000,000 in China alone, 230,000,000 in the Soviet Union, are governed by the theories of Karl Marx. The classic picture of the Communist bloc is of fourteen nations, welded together by their common ideology and by hostility to the capitalist world. Now we plunge behind the Iron Curtain to explore for ourselves.

Two Faces of
Communism

Communism, like Janus, a god of ancient Rome, shows two faces to the world. To gaze on one and then the other is to glimpse the lure and the ultimate disenchantment of this political movement which fundamentally divides the world.

Communism, wrote Milovan Djilas, begins always as a movement of "highest idealism and selfless sacrifice, attracting into its ranks the most gifted, the bravest, and even the most noble intellects of the nation." Why? Because, continued the Yugoslav leader, communism promises "care and protection for the young, and tender respect for the old . . . selfless love, comradeship, solidarity."

With all the fervor of religion, Communists tell the world that Karl Marx discovered an interpretation of history which, seized upon by men of good will, can build a society just to all. To some idealists, struggling in vain to find social justice in the world around them, this preaching breaks like a fresh dawn after night.

"The new light," wrote Arthur Koestler, "seems to pour from all directions across the skull; the whole universe falls into·pattern like the stray pieces of a jigsaw puzzle assembled by magic at one stroke. There is now an answer to every question, doubts and conflicts are a matter of the tortured past. . . ."

To the American author Richard Wright communism lighted a path toward Negro equality in the United States. André Gide, a Frenchman, traveled to French colonies in Africa and was appalled by white treatment of the natives. Privileged himself, he longed to help the downtrodden of the earth. In communism he thought he had found a way to abolish the "abominable formula, 'Thou shalt earn *my* bread in the sweat of *thy* brow!' "

These men had found a dream in the first, the alluring, face which communism shows to the world. In the German city of Berlin the Communist image is harshly different. There, on August 13, 1961, workmen of the German Democratic Republic, covered by the guns of East German troops, hastily erected fifteen miles of concrete blocks, barbed wire, and floodlights through the heart of a great city.

The Iron Curtain which had come down between Communist East Germany and the free part of that country, called the German Federal Republic or West Germany, did not directly affect Berlin. When the fighting had ended, after World War II, Berlin lay 110 miles inside the zone assigned to the Soviets. The Western Allies, too, wanted their foothold in the former German capital. So the city became a pie, sliced into four occu-

A mileage marker on the Autobahn. The bear is the symbol of Berlin.

pation sectors, like Germany around it. In 1949, when the Soviets gave up their sector, East Berlin became the capital of the Communist GDR. But West Berlin remained under Western control—a glittering, eye-catching island of the free world, deep within the Communist bloc.

The city became, in the words of former Soviet Premier Nikita S. Khrushchev, a bone in the Communist throat. Hordes of East Germans, unable to escape through the Iron Curtain, were traveling to East Berlin, their "capital," crossing freely to the Western sector, and flying to safety in the West. By the summer of 1961 more than one thousand East Germans were pouring daily into West Berlin.

Soldiers putting up cement blocks to seal off the Soviet sector in Berlin. Below: Mothers and children chat by the Berlin Wall. East Berlin is in the background.

The GDR economy, losing workers at such a rate, faced ultimate collapse. This in turn would have rocked the foundations of the satellite system established by the Soviets after the war. The Communist answer was to build the Berlin Wall, sealing off the last escape route to the West.

A death strip was cleared just east of the Wall, in the GDR sector. Mines were laid, searchlights erected. Houses along the border were bricked up or knocked down. Elevated guard posts covered every inch of the fifteen-mile barrier. Desperate people trying to flee were shot down by Communist troops. From August 13, 1961, to the end of 1966 more than sixty East Germans were killed along the Wall. Shots heard in the night may have killed more. Victims sometimes were left to bleed to death at the foot of the Wall, their cries reaching Western ears, before Communist border guards hauled them away.

The City Hall of West Berlin, where President Kennedy stood in 1963

This is the brutal face of communism, the face best known to people in the West. And the lessons of June 1953, when East German workers rose in hopeless revolt; of the Hungarian rebellion of 1956; and of the Berlin Wall were not lost on idealists like Djilas, Koestler, Wright, and Gide. Long before the Berlin Wall went up, every one of these men—bright voices of Marxism in years gone by—had broken with communism in disgust. Communist ideals, wrote an embittered Djilas, exist "only while the movement is young, before it has tasted the fruits of power." Of himself and many others Arthur Koestler says: "We ex-Communists are the only ones on your side who know what it's all about."

The highest-ranking official to break openly with communism was Milovan Djilas. A wartime partisan hero in Yugoslavia, he had risen to the nation's number two post under Marshal Tito. At the height of his career Djilas, Vice-President of Yugoslavia, was looked upon as Tito's

Futuristic convention hall is characteristic of the glittering new look of West Berlin.

natural successor. Then Djilas began to criticize the system for which he had fought so hard. Culmination was the publication in the United States of his book *The New Class*, written while Djilas was in prison for his earlier censures.

In this book Djilas explained why no Communist Party, having attained power, ever relinquished that power; why no Communist revolution ever evolved beyond dictatorship of the party. He attributed this to the rise of a "new class," consisting of those party bureaucrats who had "special privileges and economic preferences" because of the administrative posts they held.

Bureaucrats in other societies, Djilas wrote, had political masters over them, exercising a check on their activities. The "new class" was subject to no such check. Communist bureaucrats made policy and carried it out. Their power was based on "ownership" of the means of production.

Marx had taught that bourgeois exploitation of the proletariat derived from ownership of land and factories. Stripping the bourgeoisie of its property meant abolishing it as a class. The revolution had accomplished this, transferring ownership theoretically to the people. Industrial plants became known as "people's own factories." Farms became "collectives."

In fact, wrote Djilas, the people had little say in the management of these things. Authority to use, enjoy, and dispose of nationalized property belonged to the Communist bureaucracy. This new class conferred privileges on itself—cars, country houses, special bank accounts, all supposedly in line with its administrative tasks—and denied preference to those outside the class.

In East Germany I met a man who, though not a member of the party, contributed through his inventive skill to the making of fine machinery which the GDR exported. These exports earned West German marks, French francs, and other hard currencies vital to the East German economy. This man did not belong to the new class. But he helped to strengthen the economic structure on which the new class battened. Privileges ordinarily reserved for Communist officials reached out to embrace him.

His patents earned income which was taxed by the state at a relatively low rate. He was allowed to have a company car and to buy a small Italian automobile which would have cost $5,000 because of East German import duties, but he could afford it. Because he was not a trusted Communist, he could not travel to the West. But when he vacationed in Eastern Europe, he could take more money than he needed—a privilege denied to most East Germans.

In a real sense, Djilas wrote, Communist managers own property more completely than capitalists. For this new class to allow the state to wither away, as Marx and Engels had prophesied, would deprive Communist rulers of their source of power and privilege. Thus the revolution, in whatever country, became stuck, frozen at the stage of monopoly control by a ruthless party bureaucracy. The end result was despotism. The Berlin Wall is a cruel example of how far the new class will go to preserve itself.

For his heretical views Djilas was stripped of his vice-presidency, banished from the Yugoslav Communist Party, and thrown into jail. After ten years in and out of prison he was amnestied by President Tito at the end of 1966. This came at a time when the Yugoslav Communist Party, alone among the fourteen governing parties in the world, was beginning to loosen its iron control and move toward a limited form of democracy.

Few Communists were as well placed as Milovan Djilas to know what went on when a Communist Party became the government. Lesser Communists, glimpsing the truth, were afraid to speak out or, bewildered, confessed their errors in an effort to maintain contact with a party they still believed was wiser than they.

I visited an elderly woman in her cluttered little apartment in an old-fashioned, rather gloomy building on a side street in East Berlin. In the 1920's this woman had been a member of the Central Committee of the German Communist Party. Her husband had held similar rank in the Bulgarian party. Both were Jewish.

By the time I met her in 1965, this woman had spent years of her life in Stalinist concentration camps. Having fled from the Nazis to the Soviet Union, she and her husband had been thrown into jail and then moved from camp to camp. Why, she never knew.

And yet, I asked, she was still a Communist?

"Of course," she replied spiritedly. "I had only two courses open to me—either to go over to capitalism or remain a Communist. I had been one all my life. So had my father and my whole family. There was no other choice."

Had it been hard for her to maintain her faith, while imprisoned by Communists in Russia?

"Of course!" she repeated. "During the war I longed to escape to the Fascists (Germans), so at least I would know why I was being put in jail."

Hard as her experience had been, her trust in communism as a way of life had not been broken. She spoke bitterly of Communists who, disillusioned, had gone over to the West. Not for her. In the mid-1950's, after Stalin's death, she had been released and sent to the GDR. There she lived quietly on her pension—a friendly ironic woman, with large shrewd eyes and gray-black hair cut like a boy's.

In the wintry city of Rostock on the Baltic Sea I met a young East German woman. She was a mother, divorced, with a five-year-old son. She was proud of the apartment in which she lived. It was brand new, she owned it, and she could pass it on to her child.

To obtain her apartment she had joined a building co-operative in Rostock. A down payment of 1,800 East German marks ($450) had been the first step. Then she had faced a choice—either to put in 625 hours of labor on the building project or pay a sum in lieu of the work. Since she worked all day as cashier at a nearby grocery co-operative, her work on the project would have had to come at night, or on weekends, when her son needed her.

So from her small store of capital she had doled out an additional 1,250 marks ($312.50). This had erased her obligation to wash windows, scrub paint off floors, or do other chores which the co-operative might have assigned her. As it was, she and her father and mother had had to clean up the apartment after the workmen had left. Now the place was spanking clean, as a German *Hausfrau* liked it.

She showed me around—living room, a large bedroom, hallway, kitchen with stove, refrigerator, built-in cupboards, and a small but complete bathroom. The title was in her name. In perpetuity she must pay the co-operative a monthly rent of 38 marks ($9.50). That was all. For the first two years the co-operative was obliged to repair any structural defects. She could sell the apartment, though not at a profit and only through the co-operative.

New housing in East Berlin. Throughout the GDR, apartments are assigned according to need rather than party membership.

That night as we sat in her living room, warmed by a huge stove of yellow tile, there was no disposition to sell. Cozy satisfaction radiated not only from the owner, but from her parents, who had come to share the evening. Housing, her father assured me, was tight in Rostock. It was not uncommon for two families to have to share an apartment, and that was dreadful.

None of the East Germans in that Rostock room was a member of the Communist Party. Indeed, as the evening's talk waxed, it seemed clear that what politics they had was anti-Communist, though their mood was not belligerent. Here was a family of East Germans, of working-class origin or just above, upon whom a Communist government had been imposed after the war.

They did not like this. But they knew full well there was little they or their seventeen million fellow East Germans could do about it. So they had decided to make the best of it. And their dominant mood that evening seemed to be satisfaction—pleasure at their daughter's good fortune, won through her hard work and their own.

This is just what the "new class" of Communist bureaucrat in Ulbricht's country wanted. This family no longer was discontent. Housing, it seemed to me in my journey throughout the GDR, was being used by the regime as an effective tool to win compliance from the population.

Outside Leipzig, Dessau, Dresden, East Berlin, and other East German cities, new housing was springing up. Not enough to take care of everyone's needs, to be sure. But the units that were being built were assigned by the government, or by building co-operatives, according to need, not according to party membership. Faithful party members, one could assume, had no trouble getting on the right lists. But people with large families, or a workingwoman with a small child, as the mother in Rostock, also got housing, party members or not.

This was proved to me in a striking way. A young Communist and I were walking down Karl-Marx-Allee in East Berlin, flanked by tall new apartment houses made of glass, metal, and concrete. Here was one of the most prestigious avenues in the GDR. Surely, I remarked, new flats or apartments on the Karl-Marx-Allee were assigned according to party service.

The Communist looked at me in surprise. Not at all, he insisted. When I looked doubtful, he asked me to pick an apartment, any apartment, and ring any doorbell I chose. We tried one. No one was at home. I chose another and a woman's voice answered through the speaker.

"Here are two Americans," called the German Communist through the speaking tube. "We are visiting East Berlin and would like to see how people here live. May

*A view of Karl-Marx-Allee
in East Berlin*

we come up?" (Had he admitted he was an East German, the test would not have been fair.)

A hearty voice invited us up to the sixth floor. There stood a stout working-class woman, wiping her hands on her apron. "Come in, come in," she cried, as curious to see an American as I was to see her flat. Yes, she confirmed, she was a party member, but her husband, a machinist, was not. That had made no difference in their getting a flat. They had been on a housing list for years. Down the hall lived a doctor, not a party member. Their immediate neighbor was a Communist lawyer. Members and nonmembers were scattered like pepper and salt through the building, she assured me.

There seemed no reason to doubt her. The first apartment houses along Stalin-Allee, as the street originally was called, had been assigned to faithful party workers. But as Karl-Marx-Allee (quietly renamed after Stalin's demise) had developed, newer flats were parceled out with less discrimination. This reflected the regime's deliberate decision to allot housing, a family's most basic requirement, with a relatively even hand. That way unrest was lessened and people were lulled.

Some things the Communist regime cannot do. At the Rostock mother's home, for example, the coffee she served had cost nearly as much per pound as she paid for a month's rent. All tropical products, including citrus fruits, are scarce and expensive in the GDR. East Germany has failed so far to sell its own products to Africa and Latin America and cannot buy tropical foodstuffs in abundance.

Luxuries are expensive. A small East German car costs $4,000, when a citizen's name finally rolls up on the waiting list. A Volkswagen in West Germany, a better and more powerful car, costs $1,200. An East German pays $1.60 for a large chocolate bar, at least $15 for a nylon shirt, and $1.50 for a gallon of gas.

But through his factory or trade union he can take a two-week vacation on the Baltic Sea coast for about $25. Good German bread costs 12 cents a loaf and potatoes 2 cents a pound. Rents are astonishingly low. Many East Germans, like the young Rostock mother, pay $10 a month for their apartments. Larger apartments range up to $25. A leading East German professor received me in his princely home, its large rooms tastefully furnished with

Unter den Linden, a major boulevard in East Berlin, has been rebuilt in modern style.

Persian carpets and antiques. For this home he paid $50 a month.

"Up to an income of two hundred dollars a month," a Communist told me, "an East German worker lives better than his counterpart in the West. Beyond that income, the West German lives better."

A dentist in Bonn, capital of West Germany, told me he had trouble keeping a dental assistant, because one-quarter of her salary had to go for a single room without bath. He was trying to find a girl who could live at home with her parents.

Rents in West Germany are four to five times as high as in the GDR. Some foodstuffs are more expensive. But West German shops are crammed with fruits, vegetables, and canned goods from all over the world, things which the average East German cannot find at any price. Staples,

Former chancellor Ludwig Erhard talks with West Germany's first postwar chancellor, Konrad Adenauer.

in other words, are cheaper in the Communist East, luxuries either unavailable or very dear.

Communist regimes in Eastern Europe, some more completely than others, have solved the basic problems of putting roofs over most people's heads and giving them simple food and other necessities at cheap prices. In most Communist-ruled countries of Europe, the standard of living is higher than it was before the war. In nations like Bulgaria, Poland, and the Soviet Union, industrialization enriched and broadened former peasant economies.

This is no mean achievement. It has given the Communist new class time to consolidate its rule. No longer are peoples under communism in a rebellious mood. Little

Tractor assembly line at a plant in Poland. Machines such as this are helping speed up the former peasant economy of the country.

by little, however, those who live behind the Iron Curtain are expecting more; particularly youth, who, by and large, display little of the revolutionary zeal the new class would like. Through movies made in the West, radio and TV shows, from letters sent by relatives in the West, the peoples of Eastern Europe know they are falling behind the free world.

Their own eyes tell them this. Western tourists, bringing hard currency with them, are welcome in most Communist lands. Many tourists drive their cars through checkpoints in the Iron Curtain and park them at night outside their hotels. Eastern European boys and men flock to compare the latest models.

These men may not know that bicycle racks at the giant Volkswagen plant in Wolfsburg, West Germany, are empty, because most workmen own their own cars. But they do know that Western countries turn out millions of cars and that their Communist regimes do not.

The Marxist new class, having entrenched itself, cannot rest on the laurels of low rents and cheap bread. It must try to prove what communism stridently claims—that working people are better off under communism than under capitalism. If the new class cannot prove this, all its barbed wire and bayonets in the end will fail. So the new class borrows Western methods to achieve Western results. Here its troubles begin, for, when a snowball begins to roll, how large does it grow and where does it stop?

Eastern Europe
After Stalin

STALIN's death in 1953 marked a decisive turning point for the Communist world, inside and outside the Soviet Union. From 1948, when the Red Army had won Eastern Europe for him, until his death, Stalin exported to other countries the monolithic structure he had imposed on Russia.

A drive to build heavy industry; the collectivization of agriculture; persecution of bourgeois enemies; elimination of internal Communist Party opponents—these formed the steely bands of the Soviet strait jacket into which Stalin thrust the satellite lands. The aura of Stalin, the terror his name inspired, wielded by secret police in every Communist land, was the cement that held this structure together and made it truly a bloc.

Yugoslavia was a sole exception. Marshal Tito boasted Communist credentials equal to those of Stalin. Tito, even more than Stalin, had created and carried through an authentic revolution, basically without Soviet help. Now he refused stubbornly to compress his country into a Stalinist mold. Ruling an amalgam of jealous Serbs, Croats, and Slovenes, Tito claimed to know what was best for Yugoslavia.

Angrily Stalin used the Cominform, or Communist Information Bureau, to denounce Tito. A resolution of the Cominform called on "sound elements of the Yugoslav Communist Party" to overthrow the Yugoslav leader, if he failed to knuckle under. Tito's answer was defiance. In reprisal Stalin expelled Yugoslavia from the Cominform, the international organization of propaganda and espionage which the Soviet leader had established in 1947.

Every other bloc state proved sycophantic. Communists who showed signs of independence, like Wladyslaw Gomulka of Poland, were arrested. Others were killed. At the height of the Cold War, Stalin had a faithful chorus of satellites echoing his denunciations of the West, while at home these puppets of Moscow planted communism in the image of the Soviet model.

Stalin's death touched off a scramble for power in Moscow, with Nikita S. Khrushchev emerging on top. Khrushchev was a very different man from Stalin. Bald, round, with a peasant's earthy humor and love of salty proverbs, Khrushchev at times bordered on the buffoon in his public antics. Underneath, however, Khrushchev was shrewd, intelligent, and in his way as ruthless as Stalin. Lacking the aura of his predecessor, Khrushchev soon perceived that Stalin's iron grip over the Communist world could not be maintained.

Forced collectivization of farmland and blundering

Nikita S. Khrushchev, former premier of the USSR

drives to industrialize were straining the fabric of Communist rule. Czechoslovakia, for example, had been, at the time of the Communist takeover in 1948, a nation of skilled craftsmen, adept at glass blowing and other light industries. The foreign trade of this advanced society had been wrested by the Communists away from its traditional Western markets and reoriented toward the East.

Light industry was neglected in favor of heavy machine goods which the Soviet Union needed. A brief and deceptive spurt of the Czech gross national product followed.

But the price paid was resentment and finally apathy on the part of a skilled population; the Czechoslovak economy began to decline in efficiency, briskness, and dedication.

Reading these warning signs throughout the bloc, Khrushchev eased up on industrialization and began to emphasize consumer-goods production. Pointedly he curbed the powers of Stalin's dreaded secret service police. Then Khrushchev began to think out how to establish a new Communist system that would maintain Soviet hegemony, while allowing Eastern Europe to develop more naturally.

He realized that the bloc contained nations very different from the USSR and also different from one another. Khrushchev's solution was to allow each Eastern Euro-

A cotton plant in the USSR. During Khrushchev's reign, heavy industry was eased in favor of consumer-goods production.

pean state a fair degree of autonomy to develop in its own way. Khrushchev encouraged his fellow Communist chieftains to ease police terror, as he had done in Russia, and to lay stress on consumer goods, aiming toward a higher standard of living for the people. Conspicuously he cultivated *rapprochement* with Marshal Tito of Yugoslavia.

In February 1956 came a Khrushchev bombshell. Stunned delegates to the Twentieth Party Congress of the Soviet Communist Party heard Khrushchev denounce Stalin for having launched a wave of terror and "cult of personality" across the Communist world. The former godhead of world communism was ripped to shreds by his successor as an "enemy of the people." The Communist world, Khrushchev declared, must be de-Stalinized.

He scarcely reckoned on the consequences. In October of 1956 Hungary burst into anti-Soviet revolt, which swiftly spilled over into insurrection against communism itself. This was more than Khrushchev could accept. Soviet tanks rolled into Budapest, crushed the revolt, and installed Janos Kadar in power.

For two years Kadar worked to obliterate all traces of the revolt. As seen from the outside, the Khrushchev-Kadar performance in Hungary smacked of communism at its most repressive. So it was. But even Kadar had no intention of leading Hungary back into Stalinism. As soon as he could, the new Hungarian ruler slackened political controls and launched economic reforms designed ultimately to benefit the consumer.

Poland also reacted to Khrushchev's denunciation of Stalin with an "October revolution" of its own. Wladyslaw Gomulka, Stalin's imprisoned enemy, came out of

At war's end the German city of Breslau was a city of rubble. When the territories east of the Oder-Neisse line went to Poland, Breslau

jail to take charge of the Polish Communist Party. He began to return farmland to the peasants, granted new freedom to the Roman Catholic Church, and loosened the reins on Polish intellectuals.

There was no question of Poland breaking out of the Soviet orbit. "No Pole loves a Russian," observed a Polish Communist in Warsaw. "We have suffered too much from the Russians. But we Poles are realistic. The Soviets are our only guarantee against the Germans."

After World War II the Soviet Union unilaterally had annexed to itself large parts of eastern Poland. As compensation Poland was awarded former German territories east of the Oder and Neisse rivers. This gave Poland a new and uneasy frontier with the powerful German nation.

68

became Wroclaw. Above: Reconstruction has turned Wroclaw into a busy metropolis.

Many Germans still regard these lost eastern territories as German. Only the long arm of Moscow reaches out to guarantee the Oder-Neisse line. Under the circumstances, Poles have little choice but to remain faithful allies of the USSR.

Many Poles, whose hopes for greater freedom had soared in October 1956, profess bitter disappointment at Gomulka's subsequent course. Once again the regime wrangles with the Roman Catholic hierarchy. Polish writers, artists, and teachers feel the net of Communist orthodoxy lowering over their heads. None the less, Gomulka persists in unraveling Marxist doctrine by giving farmland back to private owners.

There is little contact, however, between Polish citizens

69

and thousands of Soviet troops in their country, who keep strictly to themselves. "I speak and read Russian," confided a Pole in the city of Wroclaw. "But I would not read *Pravda* on a tram. Poles would not like it." He confirmed that he never saw Russians socially, though both governments professed "fraternal solidarity."

Alarmed Stalinists in Russia and elsewhere blamed Khrushchev for the explosions in Hungary and Poland, and tremendous pressure was put on him to retrench. Khrushchev resisted. What had happened in Hungary, he argued, only proved how dangerous the bottled-up pressures had been. The only safe course was to persevere in granting the people a less anxious way of life. In 1957 Khrushchev purged his Stalinist opponents within the Soviet party, though purge in the Khrushchev era generally meant job dismissal, not physical liquidation.

Coupled with Khrushchev's internal reforms went a new foreign policy line—"peaceful coexistence" with the capitalist world. On its own merits, Khrushchev trumpeted, communism would have buried capitalism by the time his grandchildren had grown up. There was no need to foster violent revolution. Basic to this policy shift was the developing nuclear stalemate between the United States and Russia. Neither could afford war and Khrushchev had no intention of letting a small Communist nation somewhere else start a fight that Russia had to finish.

In 1962 American intelligence discovered that the Soviets secretly were installing missile sites, aimed at the United States, in Fidel Castro's Cuba. President Kennedy declared that the missiles must be taken out. Khrushchev complied and the world knew that Moscow would not risk war to extend its direct sphere of influence into the western hemisphere. In a sense this was *quid pro quo*. In 1956 the

United States had left Hungarian freedom fighters to battle vainly on their own, rather than hazard war by interfering in the Soviet domain.

"By granting autonomy to other Communist leaders," commented James Brown, chief analyst of Radio Free Europe, "Khrushchev opened a Pandora's box." He allowed nationalism and patriotism to show through the Communist mask. The old diversities which had characterized Eastern Europe surfaced again. Stalin's conformity was exposed as a short-lived aberration, a papering over of ancient rivalries.

A young German Communist and I strolled through Potsdam, whose streets were crowded with Russian soldiers, quietly shopping or sight-seeing. They walked together in uniformed groups, never mingling with the Germans around them.

"I'd hate to be a Russian soldier in my country," remarked the German youth bitterly. "If a Russian is caught even talking with a German girl, off he goes, back to the Soviet Union. What happens to him there I can only imagine."

"But you're all Communists together—" I began and the German snorted. "Maybe so, but we never talk with each other. We have to study Russian in school. Then we never get a chance to use it. Oh, we have meetings of the German-Soviet Friendship Society! They sit on one side of the room, we sit on the other." He shook his head.

Outside the East German city of Weimar lies a huge Soviet encampment. Thousands of Russian troops, including many Russian families, live behind guarded walls. One Saturday I knocked on the door of the local German-Soviet Friendship Society in Weimar. It was locked. "Always closed on weekends," said a German helpfully,

popping his head out of a nearby door. "When is it open?"
I asked. He shrugged.

Other inter-Communist quarrels have nothing to do
with the Russians. "A vacation in Bulgaria costs five hundred marks for a German from Frankfurt am Main," complained an East Berlin Communist. "The same vacation
costs fifteen hundred marks for a person from Frankfurt
an der Oder." The first Frankfurt is a West German city.
Frankfurt an der Oder lies in the GDR.

Bulgarians welcome West Germans with open arms,
for the latter pay their way in West German marks, which
the Bulgarian Government uses to buy machinery in the
free world. So West German tourists get bargain prices.
East Germans pay with the only currency they have—the
East German mark, worth little outside the Communist
bloc. The prices they pay are high. "Communist solidarity!" sniffed the East German who told the story.

"With me," said another East German, "it's not money
itself that's the problem. We have to book our tours
through our Reisebüro (government travel bureau). When
we get to a Communist country, say Romania or Czechoslovakia, we find all the best rooms reserved for West
Germans. We take what's left over."

A West German described an automobile trip he and
his family had taken through Czechoslovakia. He had
stopped at a small hotel in Pilsen, only to be told that the
inn was full. No sooner had he gotten back to his car than
the manager rushed up with apologies. He could give
them rooms, after all; he had glanced at their license plate
and seen that they were from West Germany, not from
the "comradely" GDR.

Vacations within their own country are cheap for East
Germans. But if they want to travel outside, they must

go to Iron Curtain lands. The result is discrimination, for the simple reason that Communists are avid for free world money. "Each year," remarked an East German ruefully, "we used to get wonderful strawberries from Bulgaria. They bartered these for our machinery. Now Bulgaria sells its strawberries to the West."

Other factors contributed to loosening the cement that Stalin had applied to the bloc. There was the example of Yugoslavia, which not only had defied Moscow, but was launching internal reforms that gave ideas to other Communists. Khrushchev's exposure of Stalin in 1956 had shaken many Communists, nurtured as they had been on the Stalin myth. The whole apparatus of Moscow had raised Stalin almost to the level of deity. Now the same apparatus was pulling him down. What should Communists believe?

Moscow's retreat from Cuba in 1962 did little to enhance Khrushchev's prestige in the Communist world. Peking all but called him a coward. Then, in October 1964, came Khrushchev's fall from grace. The Presidium of the Central Committee of the Soviet Communist Party announced that, for reasons of age and health, Khrushchev had retired.

To the entire world, and particularly to Communists, this was a bombshell equivalent to Khrushchev's own denunciation of Stalin in 1956. Without tipping its hand to foreign Communist parties, and without giving prior notice to the Soviet people, the Presidium had deposed the most powerful man in the Communist realm. Age and health, of course, were not the real reasons. Khrushchev had been as bubbly, as self-assertively active, just before his fall as at any other time.

This ebullience of his character provided a clue to

Khrushchev's downfall. The Soviet system, in the view of most Presidium members, had progressed beyond the need for a dynamic leader who made fundamental decisions on his own. Khrushchev's industrial reorganization of 1957 had set back the economy. His farm policies had proved disastrous. Basic to these reforms, both agricultural and industrial, had been Khrushchev's effort to strengthen party control over the economy. This conflicted with a trend increasingly visible throughout Eastern Europe—the need to put more authority in the hands of technocrats, or trained managers, who alone could guide Communist economies into the computer age.

Brilliant Soviet scientists had placed men in orbit and had developed weapons of war as sophisticated as any in the world. But the Soviet industrial record was spotty. Communist managers, inside and outside the Soviet Union, compared Soviet technology with that of the United States, West Germany, France, and Sweden and found it lacking. All this intensified the urge toward economic reform.

Czechoslovakia—though at the time subservient to Moscow—analyzed a giant American corporation to learn lessons about industrial management. East Germany and Czechoslovakia started their economic reform programs before there was a Soviet example to follow. Today Yugoslavia, Hungary, and Bulgaria, in addition to Czechoslovakia and the GDR, are ahead of the Soviet Union in reforming their economies.

The same pressing need for reform existed pre-eminently in the gigantic USSR. But Khrushchev's erratic efforts did not add up to a program. His place at the top was taken by two men—Leonid I. Brezhnev, General Secretary

Soviet premier Aleksei N. Kosygin attending a meeting at the United Nations

of the Soviet Communist Party, and Premier Aleksei N. Kosygin. The latter, significantly, had made his career as an industrial manager.

Quietly these two men began introducing the profit motive into Soviet agriculture and industry; following down the road, in other words, blazed by Communist governments in the former satellite empire. This freedom to make changes throughout Eastern Europe had resulted from Khrushchev's conscious relaxation of controls. But Khrushchev himself had lacked skill at comprehending and directing the economy of his own country.

Quite apart from its internal aspects, Khrushchev's over-throw—like his earlier criticism of Stalin—had the side effect of shaking Communist confidence in Soviet leadership. The net result was a further loosening of bloc solidarity.

Underlying all these centrifugal, or diversifying, factors was the realization of the Communist new class that national economies had to be modernized. The old Soviet model of rapid industrialization, coupled with collective farming, had sufficed to bring primitive economies farther along than they had been before. At the new level of achievement, however, further progress was being choked by slow-moving centralized control, inherited from communism's earliest days. But there was no intention of abandoning party control. The new class of bureaucrats would simply seek its ends through different means.

These means added up to a new economic policy for Eastern Europe, though this policy differed from country to country. A first step was to reorganize the economy into groups of industries, similar to holding companies in the West. General Motors in the United States, for example, owns Chevrolet, Pontiac, Buick, Cadillac, and other automotive divisions. Each operates independently and to some extent they compete with one another. But all are responsible to the same holding company.

So according to the new Communist economic policy, all chemical plants were grouped in a central holding company, whose lines of authority ran out to every chemical manufacturing installation in the nation. The same was true for other branches of heavy industry. Each became responsible to a state-owned holding company, instead of to the state itself. This was an advance toward decentralization and more efficient management.

An East German official explained to me how the system worked in the GDR. "My own VVB," he began, "embraces fifteen VEB, or People's Own Factories." (The initials VVB designate the holding company, best translated as Association of Nationally Owned Manufacturing Plants. Each plant within the complex is called a People's Own Factory, or VEB. The names vary from country to country, but the principle is the same.)

"The director of our VVB," the official continued, "is responsible to the ministry for heavy machinery and plant construction. But the director has a good deal of latitude on his own. He has, for example, a fund entirely at his disposal, from which he can pay premiums to engineers and workers for excellent results."

The manager of each VEB within the holding company also has an incentive fund, as we saw in the case of the Leipzig People's Own Factory, which manufactured railroad cranes. The new economic system thus includes two possible incentive payments, one at the factory level and the other at the level of the holding company.

"In Dresden," the chemical official went on, "we also have a testing and research institute, which does work for all fifteen plants within our VVB. Another function of the VVB is to maintain a pool of executive talent, which the director can ship out to a VEB that may be in trouble. The director also can shift, or even fire, lower executives, without referring to the government. This is new."

Each People's Own Factory keeps a part of its own profits, for reinvestment in the plant and for paying bonuses. The VVB receives another share of the profits earned by each factory, as a reserve fund to help out in emergencies. Not only in East Germany, but throughout

Poland occupies second place in the world in the production of fishing vessels. A view of the drydock in the Paris Commune shipyard in Poland.

the Communist bloc, the holding company is replacing the government as the operating center of economic power.

This by itself, however, was not enough. Formerly a Communist plant manager had been told by government planning authorities exactly how many items of his product he was supposed to make in a year. If the director was ordered to produce 1,000 typewriters and he obtained 1,100 from his workers, he had overfulfilled the norm. But if production fell short, he had failed to meet the plan.

This system was unrealistic. Since quantity and not quality was the criterion, a plant could meet its quota—and often did—by producing slipshod goods. A factory that overfulfilled its plan still might be a money loser for the state.

"To lick this," declared an official in Warsaw, "Poland switched from quantity planning to value planning. A plant manager was directed to produce, say, two million zlotys worth of goods. Formerly he had been told how many workers he must employ the quantity of raw materials he would receive, and so on. Now he can tell us what he needs to achieve his value target." Like his East German counterpart, the Polish plant manager reports to a new "industrial association," similar to the VVB of the GDR.

"We are beginning to talk of profitability as the one all-important indicator of how a plant should be operated," continued the Warsaw economist. "The manager has greater leeway to run his factory so as to produce a profit—for the state, for his workers, and for himself."

Oddly enough, the new system ran into worker resistance, for the state had planned first to plow back profits into new plant capacity and not give extra money to the people. To placate workmen, the Polish Government revised its factory bonus plan. The bonus to be paid was split into value components. A 5 per cent increase in a factory's production counted 60 per cent toward a full bonus. An accident-free year earned another 5 per cent. Adding a new item to its line of production gave a factory 25 per cent on the bonus scale, and so on. This new system stimulated workers to do a better job. "So far, however," admitted the Warsaw economist, "satisfying the workers has eaten up the profits. We have failed to increase production through new plant investment."

Formerly Communist governments had pumped subsidies into factories to keep them going. The factories had paid no interest to government on this capital. Now the new idea is for each enterprise to replace its old machinery and modernize its plant out of its own resources, to borrow as little money as possible from the government. When a factory does have to borrow, it will pay interest on the loan, as a Western firm does when it borrows from a bank. This will force Communist plant managers to use their money more efficiently. It also will establish realistically how much goods cost to produce.

Everywhere the Communist new class is striving to revive momentum in its societies, now that revolutionary fires are dying out. Police terror as a coercive has been lessened, and instead economic reform has taken its place. "Young people," declared a Western expert, "are no different east of the Iron Curtain than west. They want good living now." By offering material incentives—the profit motive—the new class hopes to modernize society and thereby perpetuate its control.

Problems remain, however, none more troubling than the bloc's basic shortage of raw materials. East Germany exports plenty of brown coal, but imports all its petroleum from the Soviet Union. Poland has the best sulfur de-

Students in the workshop of the Technical School of Oleśnica, Poland

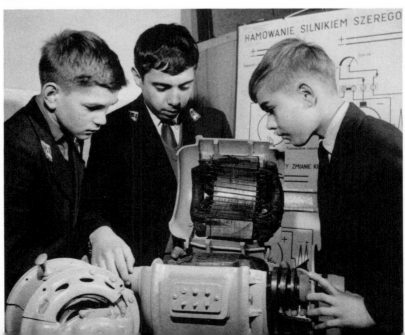

posits in Europe, but buys 90 per cent of its oil, half the materials that go into steel, and most of its natural gas from the USSR. Other bloc nations are in similar plight.

Rich in natural resources, relatively poor in modern manufacturing equipment, the Soviet Union pressured Eastern Europe into an unnatural trading pattern. Moscow would supply the raw material needs of smaller Communist powers. They in turn, particularly East Germany and Czechoslovakia, would funnel finished goods back to the Soviets.

Shrewdly the Soviets sought to deepen the bloc's dependence on Moscow. East Germany's only oil refinery is at Schwedt, close to the Polish frontier and to the terminus of Russia's Friendship Line. This vast pipeline system, more than two thousand miles long, pumps Soviet crude oil to Poland, East Germany, Czechoslovakia, and Hungary. The location of the Schwedt refinery is ideal for Soviet crude oil, awkward for petroleum from any other source. The East Germans have one potential avenue of partial escape. They are building a pipeline of their own,

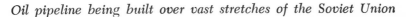

Oil pipeline being built over vast stretches of the Soviet Union

from the Baltic Sea port of Rostock across the country to Schwedt. This could be used to import Algerian or other non-Soviet crude oil.

The Soviets helped Poland build its Nova Huta steel plant. But the location is in Cracow—deep inland, where its dependence on Soviet raw materials is maximized.

This pattern of trade collides with the new economic system spreading throughout Eastern Europe. To modernize, Communist factories need new machinery. Often this can be bought only in the West. But this requires hard currency, for Western suppliers will not barter, as the Soviet Union does. Communist countries can earn dollars, pounds sterling, French francs, and West German marks only by selling their own goods in the free world, or by enticing Western tourists to visit them. Thus Poland, East Germany, Czechoslovakia, Romania, Hungary—all try to increase their exports abroad.

They do so competitively, which cuts across the trading system nurtured by the Soviet Union after World War II. Comecon, or the Council for Mutual Economic Assistance, was founded in 1949 to organize economic co-operation

A truck assembly line in a factory in Brasov, Romania

With better living standards in Communist countries, there is increasing demand for modern appliances. Inspectors check refrigerators at a factory in Hungary.

within the Communist bloc. Members are the Soviet Union, Bulgaria, Czechoslovakia, East Germany, Hungary, Poland, Romania, and Outer Mongolia. Albania, though still officially a member, does not participate. Yugoslavia has observer status, as do Asian Communist powers.

Khrushchev's idea was that each Comecon member should specialize its economy, concentrating on those things it did well. All parts then would fit together in a complementary whole. Romania, for example, should remain agricultural, to feed workers throughout the bloc. Bucharest, as we have seen, rejected this suggestion and Khrushchev's downfall killed the whole plan.

Basically, however, Eastern Europe, for political and economic reasons, remains dependent on Soviet raw materials. There is not enough money to buy oil and iron outside and, anyway, the new class distrusts the West. It wants enough foreign trade to finance Communist development, but not enough to erode the basic system. By and large, each Communist country does about 70 per cent of its trading within the bloc, 30 per cent outside.

The new Comecon concept, advanced by Khrushchev's successors in the Kremlin, is for Eastern Europe to help the Soviet Union open new sources of oil, coal, iron, and other raw materials in the vast hinterland of the USSR. Bloc nations should provide cash, machinery, railroad cars, and ships, according to their ability, to speed this development. In return their raw material needs would be guaranteed into the future.

On paper this sounds good. But it would mean tying the bloc more closely to Moscow, contrary to the present trend. Most Communist governments try to play with two strings to their bow. They participate with the Soviet Union to some extent in Comecon's mutual development plans. They also promote more trade with the West.

England, France, Italy, and finally West Germany made it easier for the Communists by offering them better credit terms. In the 1950's Western trading nations generally had agreed to limit credit to Communist countries to five years. This meant that Poland, for example, had five years to pay for machinery it might buy from France or Britain. Free world countries, by contrast, often give each other up to fifteen years to pay.

By the time Khrushchev had been swept from power and Communist governments were looking eagerly for Western trade, the five-year credit ceiling had been breached by Paris, London, Rome, and Bonn. Without going that far, the United States Government in 1967 agreed to underwrite short-term credits offered by American businessmen selling their goods to Bulgaria, Czechoslovakia, Hungary, Poland, and Romania.

Hungarian farmers stake out their land. Property formerly belonging to big landowners has been given to small farmers.

By fits and starts economic reform jerks its way through Eastern Europe, like a conveyor belt whose power keeps failing. The first glimmerings of new techniques began to be discussed in Poland in 1956, but quickly were stifled. They sprang up again, in Gomulka's Poland and Kadar's Hungary, during the next two years. A second round of momentum developed in 1963 in East Germany, the Communist world's most advanced industrial state. Today, except for Yugoslavia—which all along had pursued an independent course—the GDR has done more than anyone else to put capitalistic techniques into practice, without, of course, calling them that.

An ever-present threat to the whole reform movement is the bitter opposition of some older Communist officials, distrustful of the emerging technocrat class, who did not share in the proletariat war against the bourgeoisie. Even the boldest reformers in Eastern Europe are troubled by what is happening to traditional subsidies on housing and foodstuffs. The average Communist worker, according to the proud boast of the new class, was paying 7 per cent of his income for housing, against 25 per cent for a worker under capitalism. Artificial housing subsidies, doled out from a central treasury, made this possible. Similar subsidies kept meat, milk, bread, and other food prices low.

These subsidies were paid for by income earned by state-owned factories and farms, and by turnover, or sales, taxes paid by the people on consumer goods. Now each factory and industrial association will hold onto its profits, to finance its own depreciation costs and improvements. This means governments will lack money to pay out subsidies in the old way. What can be done?

Hungary, Poland, and Yugoslavia are experimenting with "economic" rents; high enough, that is, to cover at least depreciation costs on buildings. Since workers naturally complain about rising rents, the answer is to jack up wages to keep the 7 per cent rent ratio. But this can be done only when economic reform really takes hold and begins producing higher levels of profit. Economic reform is still too new to know whether the old wage-rent ratio can be maintained.

Another technique is to shift emphasis from state-built to co-operative housing. Apartment houses put up by co-operatives are financed by the members themselves, through cash and hours of work. As a reward, co-operative

Apartment houses in Wroclaw. New housing has been going up rapidly in many Polish cities.

members, like the young mother in Rostock, hold title to their flats. They "own" their homes.

Communist planners hope to keep retail prices at their present levels. This will prove hard, for new production techniques and the replacement of old machinery tend to make wholesale prices—the cost of producing goods—climb. The idea is to keep the consumer from feeling he is paying for these higher costs in his neighborhood store. This will require juggling with the turnover, or sales, tax.

A radio in Poland, before economic reform, may have cost the consumer 100 zlotys. Perhaps 25 zlotys of this was turnover tax, which the government siphoned off and devoted to subsidies on housing or food. Polish economic planners would like to keep the price of that radio at 100 zlotys, even though the radio now costs more to make. So

Despite increasing prices in foodstuffs, Hungarian stores display an appetizing selection.

the tax is reduced to 10 zlotys. This gives the government less income, but keeps the consumer happy. He is paying no more for his radio.

This device will not work for basic foodstuffs, which always were tax free. Since farms, like factories, are expected under the new economic policy to be profitable, collectives may be obliged to raise the price of the meat, milk, and vegetables they market. How to prevent these higher prices from being passed on to consumers? So far no answer has been found. Hungary, for example, already has raised the retail price of meat. This is a touchy problem for economic planners, arousing the ire, not only of citizens, but of the Communist old guard as well.

88

How Far the
Pendulum?

How far will the new economic reforms go before the planned economy of communism gives way to something like the free trade system of the capitalist world? Will the yeast of reform ferment communism right out of business? Almost certainly not, experts agree. Fundamental differences persist between capitalism and even reformed communism.

Ownership is one such difference. Economic reforms do not diminish state ownership of the means of production in Communist societies. By contrast factories, farms, banks, and stores are privately owned under capitalism. A "modern" Communist government may allow a factory manager to decide how he will achieve his value quota. But the government still tells the manager what his factory must produce.

Between a large American corporation and a Communist industrial plant there is one curious parallel, however. Ownership and management are separate in both cases. The American corporation is managed by businessmen on salary, responsible to thousands of stockholders, who are the real owners of the business. The Communist enterprise is managed by technocrats, who own no part of the factories they run, but are responsible to the government owner. Here the parallel ends, for the Communist government can change the management of a factory, whereas the United States Government cannot. Only stockholders, acting through their board of directors, can fire and hire the salaried managers of their business.

Also, an American company is what is called open-ended. It can move into other lines of production, buy up other companies, or go out of business altogether. This cannot be done in the Marxist system, except through the government, which means, of course, the Communist Party. Finally, governments east of the Iron Curtain still allocate the flow of raw materials and capital throughout their economies. Materials and money, except in times of stress or war, move freely in the capitalist world, obeying the laws of supply and demand.

We have discussed the centrifugal, or diversifying, factors which pulled apart the bloc built by Stalin and turned it into a "Soviet commonwealth." There is a limit to this tendency, for centripetal, or unifying, forces still exist. There is the hard fact of Soviet military presence. Today Red Army troops are stationed in East Germany, Poland, Hungary, and Czechoslovakia. But within hours they could be anywhere else in the bloc.

In 1956 Hungary tried to leave the Warsaw Pact, the military alliance which the Soviets had fashioned in May 1955 to counteract NATO. Moscow, along with crushing

Hungary's short-lived rebellion, nipped this withdrawal in the bud. The Warsaw Treaty Organization is a twenty-year alliance placing all Communist states of Europe, except Yugoslavia, under a unified military command and committing all members to one another's defense. Supreme commander of Warsaw Pact forces has always been a Soviet general, just as NATO's supreme commander is an American.

Through the Warsaw Pact, Moscow keeps a controlling hand on military forces throughout the bloc. Romania sought in vain to ease out of the pact. Albania ceased active participation in the alliance, but remains formally a member. In 1975 the Warsaw Treaty Organization comes up for revision. Until then, the forbidding shadow of the Red Army—the only force among Warsaw Treaty members in control of nuclear weapons—will exercise a restraining influence on ambitious Communist leaders in other countries. This was amply shown in August 1968, when the armed forces of the Soviet Union, plus four other Warsaw Pact allies—East Germany, Poland, Hungary, and Bulgaria —invaded Czechoslovakia, to curb the liberal reform movement launched by Czech Communist Party chief Alexander Dubcek.

No Communist leader is more ambitious than Romania's Nicolae Ceausescu. In May 1966 he declared that "all military pacts, including the Warsaw Pact, are a contravention of national sovereignty and independence." But Soviet, and perhaps bloc, pressure dissuaded Ceausescu from openly calling for the dissolution of the military alliance, at least before the disbandment of NATO.

Poland and East Germany still welcome Soviet protection against what they regard as a West German threat. This attitude contrasts with that of the "southern tier" of

Communist states, who look upon the Federal Republic as a welcome source of advanced industrial techniques. One reason Moscow invaded Czechoslovakia was to halt the spread of West German influence in Prague. Hungary and Bulgaria—though they, too, like Czechoslovakia, would welcome West German aid—had no choice but to follow Moscow's bidding and send their forces into Czechoslovakia. Romania and Yugoslavia bitterly opposed the Warsaw Pact intervention.

Whatever their national strivings, leaders east of the Iron Curtain remain Communists. None wants to see his own position, and that of the Communist Party, eroded. Indeed, they adopt Western economic techniques only to ensure Communist control into the future, not to see it eaten away.

China is a separate question. Peking claims that European Communists, led by the Soviet Union, threaten the future of the movement, by their capitalist innovations and their stress on peaceful coexistence. European Communists, with the exception of Albanians, believe just the opposite—that China's reckless course threatens war and the ruin of Communist achievements.

These opposing views led to a fundamental split between the Soviet Union and mainland China, the two giants of the Communist world. This split is couched in doctrinal terms, but includes a revival of traditional Chinese-Russian hostility. Scorning Khrushchev's policy of peaceful coexistence, Peking accused Moscow of abandoning Marxism, co-operating with the bourgeois world, and introducing a return to capitalism in the Soviet economy. These charges began to be leveled in 1956 and the quarrel broke into the open in 1960.

Mao Tse-tung's government proclaimed itself the ardent champion of revolution throughout Asia, Africa, and Latin America, particularly against the chief "imperialist" power, the United States. The duty of Communists everywhere, Peking preached, was to foment revolution, not to slide backward toward the bourgeois world, as the Soviet Union was doing.

Peking insisted that the Soviet Union wrongfully held vast border territories in Asia that really belonged to China. Maps were published to back up these claims. One day, Peking implied, China's land-hungry masses would take back these lands. Quietly Moscow transferred a number of Soviet Army divisions from western Russia to points along the frontier with China. Soviet soldiers were warned to be on guard against possible aggression.

Moscow withdrew its technicians from China, stopped aid to Peking, and did its best to thwart the latter's nuclear ambitions. As to the disputed territories, Soviet archaeologists uncovered "proof" that the areas in contention had been settled originally by non-Chinese peoples, contrary to the assertion of Peking's "falsifiers of history."

Scoffing at world disarmament, Chinese leaders professed to be unafraid of nuclear war. Everyone else might be wiped out, Peking boasted, but 300,000,000 Chinese would survive. Against this ominous background, Chinese scientists pressed on with China's own nuclear arsenal. Beginning with its first atomic explosion in October 1964, China by the end of 1966 had detonated five nuclear devices. The fourth was described by Peking as a nuclear-armed missile. In June 1967 China exploded its first hydrogen bomb, a weapon more complicated and powerful than its earlier atomic devices.

(Opposite page) Above: Chinese school children march to a mass rally staged by China's revolutionary Red Guards. Below: Formal ceremonies in which demonstrators change the name of one of Peking's streets. The new name is Anti-Revisionist Street.

Above: Well-stocked shops with a variety of products and even luxuries are found in Peking. Below: Several Chinese anti-revolutionary leaders, wearing dunce caps, are held up to public shame.

No one was more upset by these developments than the Russians. Thinly populated Asian stretches of the Soviet Union were both tempting to the Chinese and hard for Russia to defend. Moscow denounced Peking's whole foreign policy as reckless and divorced from reality. The Chinese simply did not understand, Khrushchev argued, that nuclear war must be avoided, lest everything already accomplished by socialism be undone. Peaceful coexistence was the correct Marxist line; capitalism was bound to disintegrate in time.

Other powers grew alarmed by Peking's aggressive talk. Several Arab, Asian, and African states, originally flattered by Chinese courtship, reacted in suspicion against Peking. China's leaders, wrote Professor Lucien W. Pye in *The Christian Science Monitor*, had succeeded in turning the capitalist United States, the Communist Soviet Union, and Socialist India into "their three principal, if not mortal, enemies . . . By any logic of history it would have seemed well nigh impossible to put together such a combination of enemies."

With all their reckless words, Peking's rulers were careful not to provoke a direct clash with the United States. China claims as its own the island of Formosa (Taiwan), where Chiang Kei-shek holds sway. Yet Communist China never has challenged the U.S. Seventh Fleet, which stands between Formosa and the mainland.

By comparison with China, the Communist states of Eastern Europe, even the Soviet Union, are relatively open societies. Western experts can judge with some accuracy where the Communist bloc is going. Such is not true with China. The West, and here one must include the Soviet Union, has too little evidence to know where and how

Peking's future rulers will lead nearly one-fifth of the earth's people. Against this vast uncertainty the United States and the Soviet Union cautiously explore the possibilities of co-operation.

The Soviet-Chinese split gave smaller Communist powers more freedom to maneuver. Romania, displeased by Khrushchev's ideas for Romanian economic development, began to play off Peking and Moscow against each other, spurning neither, but balancing delicately in between. Khrushchev wanted Romania to remain primarily agricultural. This was sharply rejected by Romanian Communist Party chief Nicolae Ceausescu. He intended to modernize his country and, what was more, Romania would buy the best machinery it could find. In practice this meant buying in the West.

In June 1964 Romania and the United States signed a trade agreement, as part of President Johnson's effort to "build bridges" to the East. Resulting from this trade pact were contracts for American firms to build two factories in Romania—a synthetic rubber plant and a catalytic petroleum cracking unit—worth more than fifty million dollars. Bucharest was equally zealous in building trade with western European nations, primarily West Germany. In 1966 Romania became the first Communist nation after the Soviet Union to open diplomatic relations with Bonn.

Tiny Albania, alone in Eastern Europe, espoused Peking's cause. This was inspired by fear of what Soviet *rapprochement* with Yugoslavia might mean to Albania's Communist leadership, for Marshal Tito and Enver Hoxha did not see eye to eye. Here again was a cropping up of an old pre-Communist Balkan feud, this time between Albania and Yugoslavia. Hoxha's way out was to seek

Corneliu Manescu (left), then Romanian Foreign Minister, with West Germany's Willy Brandt. Romania became one of the first Communist countries to recognize West Germany diplomatically.

Chinese protection by becoming Peking's mouthpiece in Europe.

Torn by internal convulsions as China is, no one can safely predict what damage the tail of this dragon may inflict in its thrashings. Conceivably, Moscow and Peking could patch up their quarrel and reunify the Communist world, once China's civil strife dies down. Or that huge nation might split into fiefs as in times of old, ruled by jealous Communist warlords. Or China could pull itself together, persist in a radical revolutionary course, and thereby cause European Communists, as well as capitalists, to be united against her.

One can conceive of an open alliance between the Soviet bloc and the Western world—the Warsaw Pact and NATO—against a common Chinese threat. Even this, however, might not bring about changes of governments east of the Iron Curtain.

When all is said and done, Communist governments, using capitalistic reforms for their own ends, may have set in motion forces they will find hard to control. Will economic reform lead eventually to political liberalization? It may. To become more flexible economically, to decentralize the decision-making process, would seem to lead toward similar tendencies in the political field. But not necessarily.

The East Germans, for example—leaders in economic reform—are rigidly orthodox politically. East Berlin claims economic reform has nothing to do with politics. The two are in separate boxes. This may be an overstatement, but there is something to what the Germans say.

"Remember," observed an American expert, "this growth of technocrats and managers in Communist society brings a broader base of people into authority, imbued with desire to cling to the system that brought them forward. Technocrats, though devoid of the revolutionary zeal of early Communists, none the less owe their preference to the system. They may have no 'democratic' desire to share power with the common man."

This expert went further. "In Yugoslavia and Hungary the party allows more than one candidate to compete in a constituency. Both are Communists. But they may be as different, and offer as much alternative to the voter, as Democratic and Republican candidates back home.

"Then," he continued, "in Poland and to a lesser extent in the GDR, the party uses a list system—more people on the lists than there are seats to be filled, so that voters cross out names. This, too, is a kind of choice, though totally among Communist candidates. Whether the economic reform impulse will lead to political pluralism beyond this, is still unclear."

Only in Yugoslavia is there the slightest indication that a second political party, a "loyal Socialist opposition," as Djilas calls it, might evolve. Ever since 1948, when they defied Stalin, Marshal Tito and his Yugoslav comrades have been the mavericks of the Communist bloc.

As part of their economic reforms, the Yugoslavs introduced a system called "workers' councils." The idea was for managers of a plant and their workers jointly to run an operation. Disgruntled workmen claim it doesn't really work that way. None the less, Yugoslavs direct their enterprises more "democratically" than elsewhere in the bloc.

Similarly, Yugoslav Communists are breaking with the traditional Communist concept that trade unions are captive organizations through which the party sells programs to the workers. Hungary still holds that the union's function is to oversee safety regulations and working conditions, and to report on managers if they do a poor job. But unions and workers should have no say in the management of plants.

Yugoslav unionists disagree. They claim the union should represent the workers, not the Communist Party. Many rank and file unionist, their leaders stress, are not members of the party. This view is heretical, for it would set up a center of working-class power outside the party. The argument still rages. But the liberal view gained powerful support from Veljko Vlahovic, a leading theorist of the Yugoslav Communist Party.

Marshal Tito of Yugoslavia and Nikita Khrushchev exchange greetings before a meeting of the General Assembly at the UN in 1960.

In a speech at Zagreb, monitored by Radio Free Europe, Vlahovic declared that future trade union statutes should drop the statement that the "trade unions accept the program of the League of Communists, because the trade unions are different (organizations) in which the Party program is obligatory only for Party members." (League of Communists is the formal name of the Yugoslav Communist Party.)

In December 1966 an event unprecedented in the Communist world took place in Yugoslavia. A government's proposed law was voted down by parliament and the government resigned. Such things happen as a matter of course in Western democracies, like Britain, where the government is responsible to parliament. But not in a Communist society, where parliaments, or soviets in the Russian term, are simply rubber stamps for party proposals.

It was not the Yugoslav Government itself which resigned in December 1966, but the regional regime of Slovenia, one of the six republics which make up the Yugoslav nation. The Executive Council of Slovenia stepped down because its regional parliament had defeated the council's draft law on health and social insurance.

Background to this event was the demand of Yugoslav liberals that henceforth governments should be responsible, not to the Communist Party, but to the people, through the parliaments which voters elected. This demand was voiced by Edvard Kardelj, president of the National Assembly (federal parliament) and number two man in the Communist Party. In October 1966 he had proposed in *Komunist*, the party weekly, that both the federal government and provincial regimes should resign when they lost the confidence of parliament. The action in Slovenia was the first concrete response.

Kardelj did not advocate the replacement of fallen ministers by opposition politicians. He did not want a two-party state. But he did ask for more effective Communist government, responsible directly to the people.

Early in 1967 Dobrivoje Radosavljevic, a senior official of the Serbian Communist Party, went even further. Also writing in *Komunist*, Radosavljevic proposed that Communists and non-Communists should have equal freedom of expression. If Communists were outvoted on an issue, they should defer to the majority will.

The expression of views such as these, and the resignation of the Slovene Government, sent profound tremors through the Communist world. For it was Yugoslav pioneering that had paved the way for other Communist states to institute economic reforms. Who was to say that political reforms now being argued out in Yugoslavia would not similarly creep across frontiers?

To insure that Yugoslav progress could not be undone by Communist reactionaries working through the secret police, Marshal Tito curbed police powers more drastically than Khrushchev had done in the Soviet Union. On December 9, 1966, the Yugoslav Parliament passed a "law of internal affairs," which stripped the secret police of political functions and placed the entire security apparatus under parliamentary control. This also was unique in the Marxist world.

Yugoslavia stands at one end of the Communist spectrum, beginning to discuss "democracy," though not in terms of a two-party state. The ideal, as stated by Kardelj and other liberals, would be a balanced society in which the Communist Party guided, but was subordinate to the people's will, expressed through parliament.

At the other end of the scale stand regimes like that of Walter Ulbricht in East Germany. Put in power by Soviet bayonets, backed up by twenty Red Army divisions on East German soil, Ulbricht's regime would be pulverized in a free election. So there will be no free vote, or political relaxation, if Mr. Ulbricht has his way.

China's future course will profoundly affect the Communist governments of North Korea and North Vietnam.

The same is true of Albania, since Enver Hoxha took up China's cause in Europe. In return Peking granted Albania $125,000,000 in economic credits and sent some specialists to Tirana, Albania's tiny capital.

Between East Germany on the one hand and Yugoslavia on the other, range the other Communist states of Eastern Europe. Each explores its way toward some freedom of maneuver from Moscow. Each has followed the Yugoslav example by introducing economic reforms. But all would like to keep the present dominance of the Communist Party. Can they do so? Clearly the new class is on the defensive, for Communist technocrats, striving to catch up to the West, are playing fast and loose with the "science" handed down by Karl Marx.

When a Communist Party moves too fast, or when the momentum of reform threatens to go out of control—as happened in Alexander Dubcek's Czechoslovakia in 1968 —the Soviet Union applies the clamps. But this in itself further splits the Communist world. In the long run Moscow's efforts to suppress liberalization, notably the Red Army's brutal subjugation of Czechoslovakia, may shorten the life of Soviet-dominated communism in Europe.

Failures of
Communism

At the end of 1966 wage and salary earners in the United States found an extra slip of paper in their monthly pay packets. "Effective January 1, 1967," the paper read, "the Social Security tax deduction which has been 4.2 per cent on gross pay will be increased to 4.4 per cent on the first $6,600 of gross earnings with a limit of $290.40 total deductions."

This meant that each wage earner would be taking home a bit less money to feed and clothe his family. But it also meant he would be investing in his own future, for Social Security deductions finance substantial federal payments to Americans over sixty-five. In 1965 Social Security payments were boosted 7 per cent, to an average of $80 a month for single persons and $142 for a couple. Two years later President Johnson proposed to Congress that these payments be hiked sufficiently to assure every elderly American a monthly benefit of at least $100.

Taken all together, Washington's payments to the elderly and poor—including Social Security, Medicare, educational assistance, unemployment grants, and others —amounted to more than $25,000,000,000 during 1967. The same year the Federal Republic of Germany announced social welfare payments to its 59,000,000 citizens totaling $18,000,000,000. West Germany claims to pay more per capita in social welfare than any nation in the world, Communist, Socialist, or capitalist.

These mammoth payments to the needy by the free world's richest industrial states spotlight a fundamental failure of communism—its inability to judge how capitalism would develop. When Marx and Engels wrote *The Communist Manifesto*, and even when Lenin triumphed in Russia, sweatshop conditions—the inhuman exploitation of workers—persisted in parts of the Western world.

Women garment workers stifled in New York lofts. British workers toiled over dimly lighted factory benches. Families of German, French, and Belgian miners lived in ugly coal-blackened towns. These were the proletarians about whose plight Marx wrote so indignantly. Not surprisingly he predicted violent explosions in industrial societies, ending in Communist rule.

But he was wrong. Western capitalists, spurred on partly by the specter of communism, were forced to improve conditions in their factories. Another prod was the growth of trade unions, using strikes as a weapon. Some American workers had to battle gun-wielding company police to gain and enforce their rights. Sweden's evolution into a welfare state was peaceful. In West Germany the laboring class came fully into its own only after World War II.

Whatever the route followed, the end results through-

In Socialist Sweden the elderly receive many welfare benefits. A hairdressing salon at a home for pensioners near Stockholm.

out the Western world were humane working conditions and guarantees of help to the needy and distressed. Not only had capitalists by and large ceased to exploit their workers, but the latter were sharing in the fruits of production far beyond anything Communists could match.

Average income per person in 1966 was more than $3,000 in the United States, above $2,000 in Sweden, Canada, and Switzerland, and hovered at the $2,000 mark in West Germany, France, and Denmark. Lumping together the United States, Canada, Western Europe, and Japan, average per capita income was $2,000, compared with $500 for the Communist bloc. China's extremely low

Above: A street in East Berlin. Below: A view along the Berlin Wall. At the right, in the Soviet sector, houses were torn down to prevent people from escaping into the West.

The Kurfürstendamm in West Berlin is a crowded, eye-catching thoroughfare.

income pulled down the Communist figures. Without China, the Soviet Union and its European partners earned something over $1,000 per person—half the results chalked up by the free world.

Availability of goods is another part of the picture. To buy a man's suit a Swedish worker puts in 48 hours on the job, against 153 hours for his Soviet counterpart. A television set costs a Russian 900 hours of work, a Frenchman 400 hours, and a Swiss 250 hours.

Even this does not tell the whole story. Every fifth person in the German Federal Republic is motorized. A West German need only plunk down his money to get a

Volkswagen, Opel, Taunus, or Mercedes. A Czech citizen, by contrast, waits four or five years to buy a small French or Italian car—for nearly four times as much money as the same car costs in the West.

The Czech system works like this, according to Radio Free Europe. The prospective buyer pays about $2,700 simply to put himself on a waiting list. He then waits, up to five years. He is warned his name will go behind anyone holding the Gold Star of a Hero of Czechoslovakia, Gold Star of a Hero of Socialist Work, the Order of the Red Banner, and many other awards.

Communist governments now promise that car-waiting times will be cut down—mainly because Fiat, Renault, and other Western firms have been engaged to build automobile and engine assembly plants behind the Iron Curtain.

East Germans with friends or relatives in the West can shorten waiting times for all sorts of things—if their Western friends are willing to foot the bill. This is done through a Danish company, which mails out a catalogue listing everything from cameras to cars manufactured in the Communist bloc.

The Westerner wanting to give a TV set to his East German friend deposits 825 West German marks in a Hamburg bank. This amount finds its way to an East German bank. The gift recipient receives a nineteen-inch set. The same model would have cost him 1,640 East German marks in a GDR store. Housewives shopping in East Berlin department stores find automatic washing machines priced at 2,450 marks. The same machines cost 1,320 West German marks, bought through the catalogue.

The East Germans make a car called the Wartburg. One

The Technical University in West Berlin

model costs 16,950 marks in the GDR, or $4,240 at the official exchange. Even at this price the East German customer waits years for delivery. A West German can buy the same car, without waiting, by paying 4,690 West German marks, or $1,175.

By this device the East German Government earns badly needed foreign exchange. Inadvertently, however, the Communist regime admits the weakness of its own currency and also its inability to provide enough goods for all its people.

Over and above economics, Western peoples have the priceless privilege of freedom—to vote their governments in and out of office and to move to new countries, if they choose. Millions of Italians, Spaniards, Greeks, Portuguese, Turks, and North Africans work in labor-short northern Europe, sending back money to their families at home. Communist workers, except in Yugoslavia, are hemmed in by barbed wire.

Communism never has taken root in an industrialized society, except in Czechoslovakia and East Germany, where it was established through force of arms. Large Communist parties still exist in Italy and France, smaller ones elsewhere. The Communist Party is the second largest party in France. One in five Frenchmen still votes Communist; the same is true in Italy. But these figures are deceptive, for many prosperous Frenchmen and Italians vote Red either out of habit, because their fathers did so, or in protest against other parties.

Nowhere in Western Europe, including France and Italy, do Communists have a realistic chance of gaining power on their own. The best they can hope for is to share authority through a successful coalition with Socialists.

In 1958 six Western European nations began to merge their economies through the European Economic Community (EEC), or Common Market. One provision of this market is freedom of movement for workers within the community. An Italian, for example, is free to seek a job in West Germany, or Holland. Hundreds of thousands do so and many of them vote Communist at home. Without the Common Market these men might be jobless back in Italy. Moscow denounces the Common Market as a "merger of monopolies," directed against the working class. Patently this is false, as Communist workers plainly see.

In July 1961 the Soviet Communist Party published a "new program," in which was written: "The bourgeois myth of 'full employment' has proved to be sheer mockery, for the working class is suffering continuously from mass unemployment and insecurity. In spite of some successes in the economic struggle, the condition of the working class in the capitalist world is, on the whole, deteriorating."

This at a time when France, West Germany, Switzerland, Luxembourg, Holland, and other Western European lands were absorbing millions of foreign workers, and giving them the same pay and social security benefits as domestic labor! Among the workers benefiting from this "bourgeois myth" of full employment were thousands of Communists from Yugoslavia.

In 1955 the Soviet Union began to penetrate the Arab Middle East, hitherto a preserve of Western influence. The wedges Moscow used were massive arms sales to Egypt, later Syria and Iraq, and economic development aid to these three countries. The High Aswan Dam which Soviet technicians are throwing across Egypt's mighty Nile is the area's most spectacular engineering project since the Suez Canal.

For some time it appeared that Moscow might win a secure Arab bridgehead, opening the way for Communist penetration of Africa and south Asia. But such was not to be. Arab leaders, who had fought to gain their independence from Britain and France, were not about to lose it to a new master from the Russian steppes. President Nasser of Egypt and other Arab chieftains cracked down sternly on Communists at home, even while welcoming Soviet aid.

In the first blush of the Arabs' flirtation with Moscow, some Arab governments forced their importers to buy from the Communist bloc. This did not sit well in the Arab market place. Iraqi taxi drivers liked Chevrolets, not Russian Volgas. Egyptian bakers found grit in Soviet wheat. Arab industrialists preferred American, British, or West German machinery.

Gradually the Arabs swung back toward traditional trading patterns with the West, though Soviet aid continued to flow. On occasion Communist aid technicians planned construction projects for Arab governments—only to lose the final contracts to Western firms. Cairo Radio and the Damascus press remain anti-Western and pro-Soviet in tone. But no Arab government is in danger of going Communist.

Peking had marked out Africa as its "revolutionary" pre-

Workers dig a tunnel under the High Aswan Dam. Soviet technicians are engineering this spectacular project.

serve. But the Chinese and Moscow, too, suffered sharp diplomatic setbacks in Guinea, Burundi, and elsewhere. In 1963 eighteen independent African states renewed a five-year Association Convention with the Common Market. These former French and British colonies chose to link their economies, not to the Communist East, but to the West.

Parts of Latin America and Southeast Asia still lack stability, with moderates caught in a crossfire between Communists and military juntas. Castro's Cuba became a self-proclaimed training ground for the export of Communist revolution to South America, though results so far have been nil.

Looking at the world as a whole, Communist failure to do better at home has lessened its appeal abroad. The Communist record, however, is not wholly one of failure. Most Communist governments, we recall, started in countries with underdeveloped rural economies. Western lands already industrialized had a huge head start. In per capita income some Communist nations have forged ahead of Greece and Turkey, free world members of NATO, and equal the performance of Italy. So relative backwardness behind the Iron Curtain cannot be laid wholly at the Communist door.

In his 1961 redefinition of communism, the same report in which he spoke falsely of capitalist unemployment, Khrushchev wrote: "The man-made satellites of the earth and the sun, powerful space rockets and interplanetary space ships, atomic power stations and the first triumphal orbiting of the globe, which are a source of pride to all mankind, have become symbols of the creative energy of ascendant communism."

Leaving aside his final phrase, Khrushchev had reason to be proud of Soviet space achievements. Since then the United States has caught up to and in some ways surpassed the Soviet Union in exploration of space. But Moscow's nuclear and space programs, along with those of America, remain the foremost in the world.

On a more mundane level, East Germany has fashioned a more efficient school system than West Germany, in the view of many experts. Both Germanys inherited a school system bequeathed to them by the Nazis and, before that, by the Weimar Republic. West Germany has done little to change this.

West Germany's school system, like that of prewar Germany as a whole, requires children from all social

A teacher demonstrates a lathe to young technical students in a West German workshop.

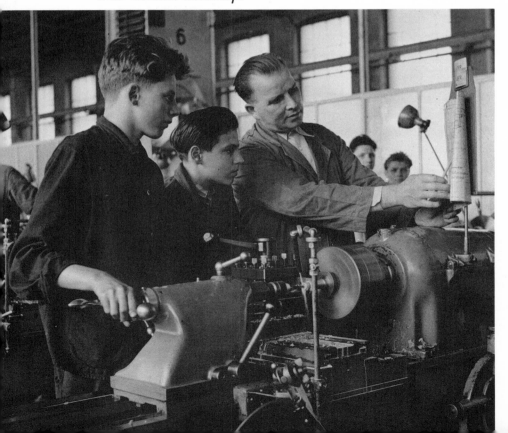

classes to sit together for the first four years of study. Then there is a division. Parents must decide whether their youngsters should go to Gymnasium (an advanced high school system), leading to university, or should continue primary schooling for four more years, to be followed by an apprenticeship or vocational school. There is a third alternative, called Realschule, or intermediate school. But this ordinarily does not lead to university.

Few working-class parents, experts claim, have the vision to launch a nine- or ten-year-old child on a school career that does not lead to a safe factory job. As a result, only 5 to 6 per cent of all students in West German universities come from worker or farmer backgrounds—about the same percentage as in the pre-Hitler Weimar Republic.

Communist East Germany, on the other hand, in 1946 passed a "Law for the Democratization of the German School." This postponed from the fourth to the eighth year a decision as to which branch of study a child should take. All children are kept together for eight years. By that time boys and girls have demonstrated whether they should go on to higher learning. The GDR reform, one West German professor told me, uncovered potential university talent which, under the West German system, often went to waste.

"An ideal education," declared a West German professor, "would be the East German school reform—filled with the content taught by West German schools." He meant that the structurally sound East German school system teaches its children communism. The "wasteful" West German system teaches democracy.

In the lovely old town of Meissen I spent an evening with an East German family, in which the mother was strongly anti-Communist. With tears in her eyes she described how American soldiers at the end of the war had fed her near-starving child. Now he sat there with us, a married man himself.

The mother told of her efforts to counteract the Communist teachings her son had absorbed throughout his schooling in the GDR. Yet in the next breath she spoke proudly of the university education he had received at the expense of the state.

The East German Government, like most other Communist regimes, guarantees each child a free education, up through the university, to the limit of the student's ability. What is more, each university student of poor family receives a government stipend, or scholarship. The son with whom I talked had been given a living allowance equivalent to $45 a month, based on his father's income.

At the University of Leipzig a student took me to lunch at the student cafeteria. Our lunch of soup, meat, potatoes, one vegetable, and a simple dessert cost 35 cents. This young man received a monthly allowance of $48. Of this amount, the student spent $2.50 a month for his room, which he shared with another student.

These benefits were not due to the boy's brilliance. He had simply passed the tests that entitled him to enter a university. As long as he maintained passing grades the state would pay his way to the end, and this particular boy would be graduated a chemical engineer. From our conversation, I judged he also would be graduated a convinced Marxist.

We have seen how Communist regimes are turning to capitalism for lessons in economics. We also have learned that Communist economics are not wholly stagnant. When

I first visited East Germany in 1964, people lamented they could not get what they needed, even if they had the money. Two years later my East German driver told me he and his wife had just bought a refrigerator and a bedroom set through a consumer co-operative to which they belonged. Membership in such co-operatives gives East Germans a chance to buy groceries, household appliances, and furniture at special prices. Periodically members receive cash rebates, based on their total purchases during the payment period.

"Our chief complaint today," reported a Communist official, "is about service industries—the repair of everything from a radio to a faucet. Finally we are producing hard consumer goods, but we are not yet organized to maintain them." He was tempted, this man confided, to do a very un-Marxist thing—to bribe a mechanic to put his Wartburg car high on the list for repair.

"But you must remember," the official concluded, "the need for service industries in itself indicates a rising standard of living. At least we now have the things that need repair."

This lack of service facilities leads Communist governments to do something else un-Marxist—to encourage private artisans to set up repair shops, particularly in small towns and in the countryside. In countries like Poland and East Germany, artisans in the past found it hard to get licenses to set up shop. Now the opposite is true. The Polish Government freely hands out three-year licenses to private shopkeepers and artisans.

These people are benefited in another way. Formerly citizens in private enterprise had been excluded from Poland's social security system. This exclusion was designed to dry up the private sector of the economy. In 1965 a law was passed putting private shopkeepers, about 200,000 people, on reduced and separate social security rolls. Long ago the Polish Government started to help private farmers plant and market their crops.

Communism's relative successes are paid for at a fearful price, from the people's point of view. That price is loss of freedom. There are some loopholes, however. Women over sixty and men over sixty-five, for example, are allowed to leave the GDR for West Germany. Also, Ulbricht's regime sells some of its political prisoners to the West. Since 1964, the West German Government has ransomed more than 150 students from Communist East Germany at a cost of $10,000 a student. This is one-tenth

In the Kielce region of Poland this blacksmith cultivates a popular metalworking tradition. The Polish Government encourages such private artisans to set up shops, particularly in small towns.

the total number of East German citizens ransomed by the German Federal Republic over the past few years.

At first, the prisoners were ransomed partly for butter, citrus fruits, and other commodities. Since 1965, however, the exchange has been strictly for cash. Most of the persons ransomed were political prisoners serving sentences in East German jails. This explains the readiness of GDR authorities to let them go. Often their "crime" had been to help other East Germans escape.

By and large, however, able-bodied persons escape from Communist rule at the risk of their lives. Recently I took a train from Pilsen, Czechoslovakia, to Regensburg, West Germany. As we crossed the frontier a high barbed-wire fence stretched away on either side into the distance. Patrolled by Communist guards, this barrier seals off Czechoslovakia from the free world.

To the north, Czechoslovak barbed wire links up with the Iron Curtain erected by the GDR. This cruel obstacle of mine fields, barbed wire, and concrete watch towers slices through Germany for 860 miles, from Czechoslovakia to the Baltic Sea. An estimated 50,000 East German troops guard the Iron Curtain. Theoretically, at least, not a single foot of this vast barrier is unscrutinized by a soldier with his gun.

Then there is the Berlin Wall, which is perhaps the ugliest proof of Communist failure to satisfy its people. "You Westerners complain about the Berlin Wall," burst out a ruffled editor of *Neues Deutschland,* to whom I talked in East Berlin. "I challenge you. As you travel about our country, you will meet many East Germans who are not Communists. Ask them, ask everyone you meet, what they think of the Berlin Wall. Then see what you think."

I did so. In Leipzig an East German professor shook his

head in exasperation. "There are so many things you people in the West do not understand! Look, for years my next-door neighbor was a doctor, the best specialist of his kind in Leipzig. One day he went West. For days his patients came to his closed door and went away, numbed at their loss.

"Many of those patients were not Communists. They were just people. Did the doctor have a right to desert them? That is why we had to put up the Wall!"

A worker in East Berlin put it another way. "Before the Wall, some of my friends in West Berlin used to come over here and shop around. A pound of meat cost them five East German marks. They took the meat back to West Berlin and sold it for four West German marks. Then they exchanged those West marks into East German marks five to one. They now had twenty East marks to repeat the process."

Some sections along the Berlin Wall are made of barbed-wire and cement-block construction.

Using the same methods, I was told, a West German could parlay a telephoto lens for a camera into a profit of a thousand or more East German marks. "Every year, through this currency exploitation," an East German economist claimed, "East Germany lost three billion marks. And it was not only West Germans who did the damage.

"Eighty thousand of our East Berliners worked in West Berlin. Let's say one of them earned five hundred West marks a month. He could change that five hundred into twenty-five hundred East marks and live here like a prince."

The Communist director of the People's Theater in Rostock was a huge man, crammed behind a tiny desk in a room below his stage. "Before the Wall," he explained, "I had no cast stability. If we developed a good actor, it was only a matter of time before a West German theater came along and enticed him over with more money. Now my

The new rolling top is part of the "modernized" Berlin Wall. The hollow pipes deny would-be escapees handholds.

actors cannot go. I can plan for the future. Who benefits? The people who come to the plays."

In Rostock, Dessau, Eisenhüttenstadt, Meissen—defense of the Wall sprang readily to lips. One reason was repeated over and over again. The flight of technical graduates to the West had to be stopped. Chemical engineers, electronic specialists, doctors—half had taken their degrees and skipped to the West. An economy drained of skill could not grow. "Who suffered from that loss?" asked a professor in Dresden. "The little people."

All right, then, I asked, what had the results been, since the Wall went up? Progress, was the prompt reply. "Our factories turn out better goods, our foreign trade has grown. Since no one can escape, the lid has been lifted on discussions. We can breathe a bit more easily."

A professor of theology with whom I spoke was hesitant, even cautious. Well he might have been, for he was a practicing Christian, teaching in an East German university. We were discussing academic freedom under Communist rule.

"Are you free," I said, "to be anti-Communist?"

"Communism," he answered, "is a form of human social life on a certain economic basis. This society needs Christ."

I persisted: "Is a young man or woman here handicapped by being religious?"

"You mean in his career?" the professor asked. "Legally, no. The Constitution guarantees freedom of worship. In practice, of course, some officials make it difficult."

"As a teacher," I probed, "what scope do you have for teaching Christ?"

One must bow to the basic system, accept it, he replied. Of that there was no doubt. But once one had demonstrated his willingness to work within the system, there was room to criticize, discuss. Room, I asked, to work for improvements, more so than under Hitler?

"Incomparably so," he replied.

I had heard the same from a professor of medicine at another university in East Germany. Racist theories had been swept away, he claimed. One could teach biology as a science.

The professor of theology fixed me with a glance. "You will find very few people here," he declared, "who like the Berlin Wall. But you will find many who will say it is necessary.

"I look at it from the standpoint of a teacher," he explained. "It costs the state forty to fifty thousand marks ($10,000-$12,000 at the unrealistic official exchange rate) to train an engineer. Before the Wall went up, more than fifty per cent of our technical graduates fled to the West. They took their education here free and put their talent to work for other people. Was that right?

"Now," he continued, "the escape hatch is closed. They work here because they must. And because they must live here, most of them do a good job. What is the result? The economy improves, the people benefit."

I told him of a family I had met in West Berlin. The father had had a good job in the East. But he had felt his son was being penalized because he was an active Christian. So the whole family crawled through a tunnel one dark night into West Berlin.

The professor of theology nodded. "I can understand that point of view. But, to me, a Christian must stand where he is and fight for his beliefs."

How hard that can be was disclosed by a young Lu-

theran pastor in an East German town. He talked to me
about the children in his Sunday school. The Pioneers, a
state organization for youth, often held meetings competitive with Sunday school, the minister said. The child who
attended Sunday school might be punished for having
missed a meeting of the Pioneers.

No child was forced to join the Pioneers, or the Free
German Youth organization for young people from sixteen
to twenty-five. But the boy or girl who did not join stood
alone. An East German schoolteacher might ask: "Which
children in the class go to church?" Officially the teacher
was not allowed to do this. But it happened. The child
who raised his hand might be taunted or—this also had
occurred, according to the young pastor—beaten up by his
classmates.

To combat church confirmation, the state had introduced the Jugendweihe, a kind of "state confirmation"
certificate. Studies leading to the Jugendweihe stressed
Marxist theory. Again, the Jugendweihe was not obligatory. But a career without one was handicapped. The
pastor said that of fifty students in his confirmation class,
only three or four were not taking the Jugendweihe as
well.

Within a certain narrow framework, what these people,
even the Communists, had told me was valid. From October 1949, when the German Democratic Republic was
founded, until August 13, 1961, when the Berlin Wall was
built, approximately 2,738,000 East Germans fled to the
West. An economy losing people at that rate could not
survive.

But this justification of the Berlin Wall required one
also to accept—as Communists do—that a dictatorship,

placed in power and held there by the Red Army and by its own East German troops, has the right to wall its citizens in. If one believes that people have a right to choose their form of government, then the Berlin Wall becomes a cruel proof of Communist failure. From this point of view, East Germany remains a prison—within which things are getting better for the prisoners.

To ease its self-consciousness, the East German Govern-

Another view of the Wall. More than 20,000 East Germans have braved bullets and land mines to flee to the West since the Wall was built.

ment is "modernizing" the Wall, to make it less ugly. The original cement blocks, topped with barbed wire, are being replaced by slabs of concrete, nine feet tall, attached to steel pilings, driven into the ground. At some points hollow pipes, which revolve at the slightest touch, are set lengthwise on top of the concrete slabs. These are designed to deny would-be escapees handholds and to hurl them backward to the ground.

More than 20,000 East Germans have braved bullets and land mines to flee to the West since the Berlin Wall went up. Most of these people ran the gauntlet, not in Berlin, but through the Iron Curtain in rural Germany. Among the escapees were more than 2,000 East German soldiers and policemen, who could not stomach orders to shoot down their fellow citizens. Other hapless Germans—more than 120—were killed during the same period, trying to escape.

The Soviet Union drove home the point of Communist failure when it invaded Czechoslovakia in 1968. The danger, from Moscow's point of view, was that liberal ideas launched by Mr. Dubcek—including an end to press censorship—might percolate northward into East Germany, Poland, and the Soviet Union. This, in turn, would threaten Soviet hegemony in Eastern Europe and, possibly, the rule of communism itself.

Red Army invaders claimed to be protecting the Czechs and Slovaks against "counterrevolutionary forces." In fact Soviet tanks were giving evidence of communism's essential failure: it must keep its people in chains, lest they forsake the Red flag.

Democratic
Socialism

THE TEACHINGS of Karl Marx produced a second offspring, called socialism. This word is tricky, for Communist officials speak of their realm as the "Socialist camp," or bloc. They also describe socialism as a stage on the road to communism. But this is not at all what Westerners understand by the word socialism.

Deriving from Marx as it does, the Socialist platform has superficial resemblance to that of communism. Socialists are more or less devoted to public ownership of some productive resources, coupled with extensive social welfare programs to help needy segments of the population. They tend to favor heavy taxation of the rich, though they do not advocate abolition of private property. Socialists also urge economic planning by government. Clearly, Socialists are for the "little man." Trade unions in Western Europe often are affiliated with the Socialist parties of their countries.

All this has given rise to the stereotype that a Socialist is "pink" and a Communist "red." Place Socialists in power and they will tend to turn redder. History indicates otherwise. Socialists are democratic, Communists are not. Socialists believe in evolution, not revolution. They do not sponsor the overthrow of government by force. Like other democratic groupings, Socialist parties campaign for people's votes. If they lose elections, Socialists go into loyal opposition.

We see this by example. In 1965 the Norwegian Labor (Socialist) Party lost national elections and went out of office, after governing Norway nearly continuously since 1935. Great Britain, Sweden, and Denmark are free world powers currently governed by Socialists. Socialists share power in the German Federal Republic. Not one of these nations is friendly to communism. Britain, Norway, Denmark, and West Germany are members of NATO. Socialists in Australia and New Zealand have moved in and out of office, without changing their anti-Communist stance. Both New Zealand and Australia belong to SEATO, the free world's collective defense pact in Southeast Asia.

Communists bitterly assail democratic Socialists, for the latter offer an alternative to the workingman, exclusive of the Communist Party.

Socialism was a familiar word before Karl Marx and Friedrich Engels began to publish their writings. The British followers of Robert Owen formally adopted the name "Socialist" in 1841. Owen and other early reformers, notably Saint-Simon and François Fourier in France, maintained that social, or public, ownership of the means of production was the only way to halt capitalistic exploitation of the workingman. To Saint-Simon, the state's duty was to take over, organize, and plan the development of a nation's economy, assigning a key role to scientific and industrial experts. The Communist technocrat of today is an extension of Saint-Simon's concept.

Both Owen and Fourier urged the practical application of their teachings through the formation of co-operative villages, which would become testing grounds of Socialist theory. An American village of this type, deriving from Fourier, was called Brook Farm, near West Roxbury, Massachusetts. This brief venture in communal living, organized by American writers and idealists in 1841, is described in Nathaniel Hawthorne's *Blithedale Romance*. Other co-operative villages based on Owenism had been founded even earlier in England, Scotland, Ireland, and other areas of the United States.

Israel is one place in the world where such co-operative ventures still flourish. Many years ago Jewish Zionists in Eastern Europe, dreaming of a return to the "Promised Land" of Palestine, evolved the concept of kibbutz, or collective, as the ideal social unit for resettlement in Palestine. Each kibbutz was to be a collectively owned agricultural village, within which Jews from European ghettos would strike down their roots in the land of their fathers, while reclaiming fields and laying the groundwork for future waves of immigration.

The first kibbutz, called Degania, was founded in Galilee in 1909. Today more than two hundred kibbutzim dot the State of Israel. Each kibbutz is affiliated with a political party, for which all members of the kibbutz vote in common. But all kibbutzim, of whatever political persuasion, share the same principles of communal living. In these kibbutzim one finds traces of socialistic concepts

Above: **General view of a kibbutz in Israel.** *Below: Workers are assigned their schedule for the coming day.*

Above: Workers in the kibbutz eat in this large dining hall. Below: Children are cared for during the day in this special house in the kibbutz.

promulgated more than a century ago by Owen and Fourier, and even earlier by the Frenchman François Noel Babeuf.

Feargus O'Connor, Louis Blanqui, Pierre Proudhon, and Ludwig Feuerbach were other European thinkers attacking the evils of capitalism and championing various Socialist solutions during the first half of the nineteenth century. It was in this dawning ambience of Socialist agitation that Marx and Engels began their work. They came upon a stage already full of actors, but it was not long before Marx stood at the center of the stage.

Those who had gone before him, dreaming of socially perfect worlds, Marx scorned as "utopians," divorced from reality. Utopia was the name given by Sir Thomas More to an imaginary island, whose inhabitants had learned to govern themselves in perfect harmony. The work of earlier Socialists, even those who had founded co-operative villages, Marx termed utopian, or idle.

Marxian socialism, by contrast, was "scientific." That is, Marx wanted to use the power of the proletariat to crush the bourgeois state. He would work *through* the working class, using its muscle to carry out the revolution. Others, by and large, had worked *for* the working class, in a vacuum of power.

The Communist Manifesto of 1848 marked the great dividing point of Socialist history. Earlier idealists had tossed up ideas which Marx later used. But only after 1848 did socialism emerge as a potent international movement, based on the teachings of Karl Marx. Even after the movement split, with the Communists and the democratic Socialists each going their separate ways, both sides continued to look back toward Marx for common inspiration.

A major step toward crystallization of the Socialist

movement was the formation by Marx in London in 1864 of the International Workingmen's Association, or First International. By 1871, when Marx had consolidated his leadership of this association, the First International had branches in most Western European countries. These branches embraced various Socialist schools, not only that of Marx, and this proved the undoing of the First International.

In 1871, following the defeat of France by Prussia, thousands of workingmen, including French members of the First International, had seized power in Paris and proclaimed a sovereign city government, called the Paris Commune. The revolution was short-lived, lasting only a few weeks before the uprising was crushed. In the process the Paris Commune exposed a basic split within the Socialist camp.

Marx and his followers later criticized the Communards for having failed to crush the "bourgeois" state more thoroughly. Other Socialist spokesmen disagreed. They held that the bourgeois state should not be destroyed, but rather conquered and then used as an instrument of power. Torn by this dispute, the First International collapsed.

Among the more moderate Socialists were followers of Ferdinand Lassalle, who had founded the first German Socialist party in 1863. Also active in Germany were two disciples of Marx, Wilhelm Liebknecht and August Bebel. In 1875, to effect a union of German Socialists, Marxists deferred to the view of Lassalle's followers that the bourgeois state should be conquered and used, rather than destroyed. The resulting compromise, called the Gotha program, led to the formation of the German Social Democratic Party.

Marxists were in control. Yet they had resigned themselves to winning political power through legal means. Despite the bitter protests of Marx himself, German Social Democrats launched themselves as a parliamentary party, not as a revolutionary force. The significance of this emerged in later years, when Social Democratic parties throughout Europe formed themselves largely on the German model.

Socialist parties appeared in France in 1880, in Belgium in 1885, and in Spain in 1879. Throughout Scandinavia, where socialism was to triumph in the twentieth century, Socialist parties had been created in Denmark, Norway, Sweden, and Finland by 1899. The Italian Socialist Party emerged in 1892, as did the Socialist Party of Poland. Under the name of Emancipation of Labor, a Russian Socialist party was founded by Georgi Plekhanov and Pavel Axelrod in 1883.

Attempts to organize a British Socialist party led to jockeying among splinter groups, until, in 1893, the Independent Labour Party emerged under the leadership of Keir Hardie. This group drew to itself trade union support and adopted an evolutionary Socialist program, opposed to violent revolution.

Ten years earlier a remarkable group of British intellectuals, dominated by George Bernard Shaw and Sidney and Beatrice Webb, had founded the Fabian Society. This organization, established the year Marx died, certainly would have been labeled utopian by the author of *The Communist Manifesto*. The Fabians, through their published essays, argued that socialism must be achieved gradually, by capitalizing on practical possibilities. Fabians advocated state control of the conditions of work and also public ownership of industry. Their theories on the development of a "welfare state," serving the "greatest happi-

Drawing of an early meeting of the Fabian Society. From left to right: George Bernard Shaw, Beatrice and Sydney Webb, and Graham Wallas.

ness of the greatest number," colored the policies, not only of the British Labour Party, but of democratic Socialist parties on the continent.

By the end of the nineteenth century, Socialist parties were going concerns throughout much of Europe. Their leaders considered themselves disciples of Marx; the language they used was Marxist. Yet most of these same Socialits, particularly in Western Europe, had turned their backs on revolution. Why this split with Marx and Engels on tactics?

The explanation is partly political, partly economic. Political conditions in Western Europe allowed Socialists to campaign openly for votes. The natural route to power, and hence to transformation of society, appeared to lie through parliamentary means. Thus Western European Marxist parties took the legal fork in the road. In Poland and Russia, by contrast, Socialists were forced underground by the existing regimes. Perforce they became conspiratorial.

Typifying the outlook of Western Socialists was Edouard Bernstein, a German who had been greatly influenced by Fabianism while working in London as a correspondent of the German Social Democratic paper, *Vorwärts*. In his book, *Evolutionary Socialism*, Bernstein denied the Marxist thesis that capitalism was headed for collapse. Nor could the proletariat by itself seize political power. Marxists, he maintained, should work within a parliamentary framework for immediate social reforms. Marxism, in other words, should be revised to conform to changing conditions in the West.

Bernstein's theses were challenged by orthodox Marxists in Germany. In fact, however, the German Social Democratic Party, while clinging to the letter of Marxism, acted increasingly in line with Bernstein's proposals.

Despite this widening split within the ranks of European Marxists, the various national parties in 1889 established a Second International Workingmen's Association, or Second International. The defunct First International had sought to impose a uniform program on all Socialist parties. The Second International was a more modest link between independent Socialist parties, each of which shaped its policy according to conditions at home.

In 1912, as the shadows of war darkened over Europe, a Socialist congress at Basle called on the proletariat of all nations to strike for peace. The appeal failed and, when World War I broke out, Socialists in the main rallied to their national flags like other citizens. French and German

Socialists, for example, fought each other bitterly in the trenches of Verdun. When the war ended, the world of socialism had changed forever, for Lenin's Bolsheviks had seized power in Russia in the name of Marx.

Breaking with Social Democrats, Lenin proclaimed the formation of the Third International in 1919, designed to foment world revolution on the Communist model. He had broken with Social Democrats and they had broken with him. Pro-Soviet Marxists in Western Europe quit the old Socialist parties and formed Communist parties, loyal to Moscow. After World War II, when Stalin exported communism beyond Russia's borders, socialism of the Western kind disappeared completely in Eastern Europe, smothered by monolithic communism.

Profound social upheavals caused by World War I brought new opportunities to Western Socialist parties, which before the war had been minority groups. Although Socialists had fought loyally on both sides during the war, Socialist philosophy generally had been pacifist. This allowed German Social Democrats to accept more gracefully than other Germans the restrictive Treaty of Versailles. Social Democrats played a dominant role in the postwar governments of the German Weimar Republic. In England, a reorganized Labour Party formed England's first Socialist government in 1924.

Social democracy had come into its own as a major political force throughout much of Western Europe. However, having decided to work within existing state frameworks, Socialists in effect were forced to "administer capitalism," in the words of Professor Joseph A. Schumpeter of Harvard.

Political conditions had brought Socialists to power,

while leaving the old capitalist economic structure intact. Socialists, wrote Professor Schumpeter, "might regulate [the economic system] in the interest of labor, squeeze it to the point of impairing its efficiency—but they were unable to do anything specifically socialist. If they were to run it, they would have to run it according to its logic. They would have to 'administer capitalism.' And this they did."

The necessity to do this sprang from Socialist acceptance of the thesis, advanced originally by Lassalle, Berntein, and the Fabians, that capitalism's economic structure should be used, not destroyed. Inevitably this alienated Leninists and made room for Communist parties to spring up in Western Europe.

We have seen how today's Communist governments, having decided to initiate economic reforms, are sailing into waters as yet uncharted. Something of the same sort happened to Social Democrats after World War I. Moving in and out of governments, like other parliamentary parties, Socialists in Western Europe gradually dropped their Marxist bias. Their redness became pink and even this turned pale. Why?

Because "capitalist" parties of the center, competing with Social Democrats at the polls, perceived that they, too, must begin to look after the interests of the workingman. Creation of a welfare state became an accepted policy plank of non-Socialist parties. This forced Social Democrats in turn to soft-pedal their Marxist origins, which still antagonized many voters.

The German Social Democratic Party was a case in point. Though moderate in action, the party clung formally to Marxist language. For many middle-class Germans this

blurred the distinction between Socialists and Communists. German Socialist workers, for their part, found it
hard to overcome their instinctive prejudice against
"capitalists." The result was hostility between Social Democrats and center parties—though both were threatened
and finally overwhelmed by Hitler's Nazis.

After World War II the Social Democratic Party (SPD)
was one of three major German political groups licensed by
the Western Allies, the others being the Christian Democratic Union (CDU) and the Free Democratic Party (FDP).
Not yet, however, were Social Democrats ready to shake
off Marxist slogans of the past. As a result they stayed in
the political wilderness from 1949, when the German Federal Republic was founded, until December 1966, when
SPD leader Willy Brandt finally led his party into a coalition government with the Christian Democrats.

To understand the Social Democratic dilemma during
these wilderness years, let us compare the rival social
security systems of West and East Germany. Above all
Communists should be able to provide top-notch protection of the workingman and his family from birth to death
—if, that is, Communists live up to their promises. For
why else did communism come to power? Yet the East
German worker is palpably worse off than his West German counterpart, not only in ownership of cars, TV sets,
and electric razors, but in many aspects of social security.

Wages and salaries in West Germany are higher than in
Communist East Germany. This means that retirement,
sickness and accident insurance, and other benefits—based
on a percentage of income—are higher for West German
workers than for their counterparts in the GDR. In 1966,
for example, Bonn paid about $1,170 to each old-age

pensioner, while the average elderly person in East Germany received roughly $450.

East and West Germans contribute their share of social security costs in different ways. The Communist program is centrally run, and about 10 per cent of the base pay of each citizen is deducted to cover all parts of the program. The West German program, on the other hand, is administratively split among many agencies. Consequently several individual slices are taken from the West German's pay packet. These, added together, total about 12 per cent. This is a slightly larger slice than that given up by the worker in the East. But the West German citizen gets back correspondingly more.

In philosophy, West German social security is strikingly different from that in the East. Every West German worker up to a certain monthly income is covered equally, regardless of his politics or occupation. Independent courts guarantee him justice, should he feel his government has treated him unfairly. East Germany, by contrast, scales social security payments according to the occupation of the insured. The worker whose skill is urgently needed receives a higher benefit than a worker whose labor is marginal. Further, the East German citizen has no independent court system through which to challenge his government's interpretation. The same agency which pays social security determines the scale.

What a feather in the cap of West German Social Democrats, if they could take credit for introducing a social welfare program that outdistanced the Communists'! But the irony is, most of this program was enacted by a "bourgeois" government, under the leadership of the Christian Democratic Union. By supporting the program in Parliament, and by goading on the CDU, Social Democrats certainly contributed to social welfare in West Germany. But credit for Bonn's program went primarily to the Christian Democratic Union, a "capitalist," free enterprise party. Capitalists had stolen the thunder of Willy Brandt's SPD.

(In 1881, when "Iron Chancellor" Bismarck governed in Berlin, Germany began to enact social welfare laws. Socialists at the time charged the bourgeois government with trying to soothe workers and head off a Marxist revolution. One way and another, German Socialists never did get credit for social welfare.)

Today West German social security, as a percentage of government spending, has about reached the limits the nation's economy can support. Even if they formed a government by themselves, Social Democrats could not add to the program. They might tinker with the machinery, adjust it here and there. But social welfare in West Germany would remain roughly what Christian Democrats had made it.

In the early 1950's, meanwhile, the Social Democratic Party was undergoing an internal metamorphosis. Outwardly the party still waved a Marxist, though strictly democratic, flag. The SPD opposed German rearmament and dug in its heels against the progressive integration of the Federal Republic in an openly anti-Communist alliance. Behind the scenes, however—prompted by Fritz Erler, Herbert Wehner, and Mr. Brandt—the Social Democratic Party was overhauling its cargo of slogans.

Culmination came on November 15, 1959, when an SPD congress—by 324 to 16 votes—adopted the so-called Bad Godesberg program. This program, in effect, accepted the government's close alliance with the West. Already SPD leaders had come around to supporting West German re-armament. Mr. Erler had worked with the CDU to insure civilian control of the Federal Republic's emerging armed forces. The main body of the SPD firmly backed NATO. In economic affairs, the Bad Godesberg program acknowledged the role private enterprise played in providing rising social welfare standards for everyone.

Having shed its Marxist cloak, the SPD began to prosper at the polls. By 1967 the SPD governed alone or shared power in six of West Germany's eleven Länder (states). As one of the two great parties of the Federal Republic,

Willy Brandt (left), chairman of the Social Democratic Party, seals the new "grand coalition" with the Christian Democratic Union by shaking hands with chancellor Kurt Georg Kiesinger.

Kurt George Kiesinger, Chancellor of the new coalition government of West Germany.

the Social Democrats joined the Christian Democrats in a "grand coalition" government in Bonn in December 1966. The CDU still was in charge, with Kurt Georg Kiesinger as chancellor. But Mr. Brandt, chairman of the SPD, was vice-chancellor and foreign minister, and the Social Democrats held eight other ministries.

Social democracy had come a long way in West Germany, but at what price? The party of Lassalle and Bernstein, Bebel and Liebknecht, Erler and Brandt, had turned essentially bourgeois. Before German elections in the fall of 1965, a party official discussed SPD policy on a range of foreign problems—French President de Gaulle and NATO, the Soviet Union and Eastern Europe, and East Germany.

"Where," I asked, "does all this differ from the policy of Gerhard Schröder?" (Mr. Schröder at that time was CDU foreign minister of the Federal Republic.)

"Really nowhere," the Socialist admitted. "It's a matter of nuance. We would stress some things differently."

No doubt they would. By and large, however, the two great West German parties see eye to eye on foreign policy. In domestic matters, too, the differences between them are small.

Other Social Democratic parties throughout Western Europe traveled down much the same road as the German SPD. Having cast off Marxist trappings, they found their field of action on social welfare progressively pre-empted by bourgeois parties of the center. A notable exception was Scandinavia, where Socialists gained office early, bringing social welfare with them.

The Middle Way— Sweden and Britain

Late in the nineteenth century Sweden sent thousands of immigrants to the United States, because their cold northern homeland could not feed them. Today Sweden, a nation of eight million people, is the most prosperous country in Europe.

Sweden has one car for every four persons. France, West Germany, and Britain have one for every five. In 1965, 440 of every 1,000 Swedes owned telephones. The comparable figure for Great Britain was 183, West Germany 139, France 117. Swedes own more television sets per capita, read more newspapers, earn more money— $2,700 yearly—than any other people in Europe.

But Stockholm also has more youngsters dressed like beatniks—boys with long hair, girls in miniskirts and leather jackets—than this writer has seen in Paris, Rome, Warsaw, or Berlin. Why?

A leading Swedish official threw up his hands. "My sixteen-year-old son wears long hair and dresses like a beggar. I don't like it, but what can I do? He says to me: 'Dad, if I dressed normally, I'd only circulate in our social class. I'd be shut off from so many interesting people.'"

The official leaned across his desk. "Right now we're having a teachers' strike," he told me. "My boy with the long hair took over and organized the work of his school class. I can't say he lacks drive and purpose."

"Many of the kids you see lounging on the streets at night," asserted another Swede, "come from upper-class families. They're protesting."

I could believe their social origins. At Stockholm's glittering opera I had seen youths in evening attire with hair flowing to their shoulders. It was easy to imagine them on other nights prowling Stockholm's foggy streets in tight pants and pea jackets.

But protesting? Against what? "Dullness," declared a foreign observer bluntly. "This country has solved its major problems. There's a sense of emptiness in Swedish society. Youth demands involvement, so it protests in the form of a beatnik outlook."

A Swedish trade union leader disputed this hotly. "We spend fifteen billion crowns yearly on social welfare. Of this, six billion crowns go to old-age benefits, another six billion for sickness and hospital payments. So when critics complain that social welfare robs people of incentive, whom do they mean? Old and sick people? That's where the money goes."

Sweden, in other words, like most other nations, is a bundle of contradictions. Thousands of American women clean their homes with Swedish-designed vacuum cleaners.

Farsta, Stockholm's newest satellite city, features a shopping center dominated by three large department stores, civic youth centers, a library, and medical and dental centers.

Two Swedes invented a principle of refrigeration still widely used. This nation of eight million people makes some of the world's most advanced jet fighter planes. Sweden has an active civilian nuclear industry, which could produce atomic weapons in a matter of months. Stockholm's department stores are among the finest in the world.

Yet Sweden's churches are almost empty. "Every Swede is born a member of the state Lutheran Church," a Swedish official told me. "But less than ten per cent are active churchgoers." Swedes trail only Yugoslavs and Poles in consumption of alcohol, according to official statistics.

Since 1932 the Social Democratic Party has governed Sweden, either alone or in coalition. Swedish Socialists

Old cultural traditions still live in parishes around Lake Siljan, a popular tourist district in Sweden—but many of Sweden's churches are almost empty.

have been in office longer than any others in the world. They have made Sweden a synonym for socialism in action. What, then, does this prosperous, sophisticated, Socialist-governed nation show?

"There seems to be a strange confusion," observed Curt-Steffan Giesecke, "between a social welfare state—acting as an insurance company to protect the citizen—and the organization of economic life. Sweden is a private enterprise land."

Mr. Giesecke is managing director of the Swedish Employers' Confederation (SAF), the organization of industrialists which bargains with Swedish trade unions. These private employers hire 90 per cent of all Swedish workers. Only one-tenth of the nation's economy is nationalized.

This is the first fact to understand about Swedish socialism. In a Marxist sense, Sweden is not Socialist at all. The Social Democratic Party has no program of nationalization. This should not surprise us, having traced what happened to West German and other European Social Democrats. Properly named, Sweden is a social welfare, not Socialist state.

The belief that the individual's welfare is the responsibility of the state is deeply rooted in most Swedes. An unmarried mother, for example, stands a better chance of getting an apartment in housing-short Sweden than a married couple without children. To Swedes this seems natural. The girl's baby pre-eminently needs the protection of the state.

This illustrates the determination of Swedes that every citizen in need shall have the protection of a benevolent

A modern play school near Stockholm

state. What in the Swedish character caused social democracy to flourish? "We are a homogeneous people," explained Mr. Giesecke. "Our social origin was farmer stock. Some of us became workers, others employers, but class lines are indistinct. Today there are few very poor people here and few very rich."

"Industrialization came late to Sweden," a diplomat offered. "The sweatshop with its social tensions did not exist. The Social Democrats were not fighting from a platform of reform. This, plus the homogeneous population and the urge to consensus, did the trick."

Consensus, or voluntary agreement, is a word heard often in Sweden. Government by consensus is the Swedish way. All parties are consulted, sharp edges rounded off, compromises reached, within the framework of a social welfare state. Pillars of Swedish social welfare are extensive social benefits, minimum nationalization, and the maintenance of full employment.

Politically, a policy of full employment is hard to argue against. Some Western specialists believe, however, that such a policy is self-defeating, since it involves artificially creating work for the unemployed. This in turn puts increased demand on resources and finished goods, causing prices to rise. The result can be loss of purchasing power for all, hitting the working class hardest.

This can be seen in Sweden. During the mid-1960's Sweden had an inflation running at the chilling rate of 8 per cent yearly. An item costing $100 at the beginning of a year cost $108 at the end. Simply put, this resulted from full—almost overfull—utilization of Sweden's resources, human and natural. "When unemployment disappears," one economist stressed, "the price of labor goes up. Employers bid for workers, so production costs rise. So do prices."

Throughout the economy wages have been rising about 10 per cent yearly. Wage agreements reached between employers and trade unions may not be inflationary themselves. But in Swedish mechanical trades about 70 per cent of all work is paid for at piece rates. If production speeds up, take-home pay is higher. This, coupled with the clamor of fixed-wage workers to catch up with their piece-rate colleagues, makes for a "wage drift" upward.

Also adding to the price rise is a 10 per cent sales tax tacked on to almost every item Swedes buy, even restaurant meals. Only exports and raw farm products are exempt. This tax, though it had the side effect of raising prices, was needed for another reason—to help pay for the nation's massive social welfare program. Having committed itself to cushioning its people against risk, Sweden also was committed to higher taxes to pay the costs.

A man earning $14,000 with wife and two children in the United States takes home $11,968 after taxes. His Swedish counterpart ends up with $8,120. A Swedish worker finds his wage increases eaten up by price climbs, the 10 per cent sales tax, and the higher income tax he must pay on his new pay raise. Income taxes are graduated more steeply in Sweden than in the United States. Corporations, in addition to their direct contribution to pension funds, pay huge local and national income taxes. These scoop off 50 per cent of corporate net profit.

Sweden recently displaced Canada as the second most prosperous nation in the world, after the United States. But inflation and high taxes are part of the price Swedes pay for full employment and huge social benefits.

Consensus has produced Sweden's "middle way"—a marriage of private enterprise and the welfare state. The Social Democrats, Conservatives, Liberals, and the Center Party—Sweden's four democratic parties—agree on the main outlines of the "middle way." This might sound like the West German example already cited, except that it is the other way around. In the Federal Republic it was Christian Democrats, or conservatives, who "married" free enterprise and social welfare, while German Social Democrats were in opposition. In Sweden the marriage was introduced by Social Democrats, with the other parties in opposition.

An example will show why the "middle way" costs so much money, and how it reduces risks for the Swedish worker. Vital to the functioning of Sweden's rich economy is a government regulator called the Labor Market Board (LMB). Commanding a budget of a billion crowns ($200,-000,000) yearly, this board strives to move workers around the map of Sweden according to the economy's needs.

Over the next few years, for example, one-third of the nation's forestry workers must be channeled to other fields of endeavor as inefficient lumber, paper, and pulp plants are closed down. Most of these displaced workers will choose new job opportunities, train for them, and resettle their families through the LMB. None of this is coercive, for Sweden—though an advanced welfare state—is completely democratic.

Each year about 800,000 workers, one-fourth of the nation's labor force, utilize services of the LMB. A forestry worker may learn through the board's weekly magazine, which lists all known vacancies and training programs, of job opportunities in Göteborg's shipbuilding industry.

The LMB pays for a trip by the man and his wife to look over conditions in the shipyard area. If they like what they see, the board moves their furniture, gives them $400 to resettle, and retrains the worker in needed skills. This last may be done directly through an LMB training program or by paying the man's new employer a stipend to train the former lumberman.

Municipal governments place 10 per cent of all new apartments at the disposal of the Labor Market Board for workers being moved. In addition the board itself owns eight thousand rooms of prefabricated bachelor quarters, which can be shifted about the country. The board now seeks government permission to build and "stockpile" prefabricated family housing.

A factory-made staircase is ready for a crane lift in this prefabricated apartment house in Sweden.

Simple restlessness will not qualify a worker for this manifold help. He must be unemployed or facing layoff or be willing to move to an area where labor is critically short. Firms are required to inform the LMB of impending layoffs at least three months in advance. Committees then are formed of local officials, LMB representatives, and employers to create, if possible, new industry in the area. The board helps by paying grants or loans to municipal governments to put up local plants. Businessmen also are reimbursed for the cost of training new workers.

"The whole process," declared Nils Kellgren, board economist, "is very flexible, adapted to circumstance. The board works as a kind of temperature control over the entire economy."

A tragic result of layoffs, Mr. Kellgren said, was the inability of many older workers to readjust, despite proffered help. Thus the labor board had begun to create "sheltered work."

Older people, both blue- and white-collar workers, were found jobs in government-owned facilities—museums, libraries, office buildings. Receptionists in government buildings often fell in this category. So far, the economist added, "sheltered work" had been found for about 12,000 people. This was .05 per cent of the Swedish labor force. About 2 per cent of the force was in need of such help. Wages of these people were paid directly by the LMB.

The labor board is equally at the service of government, employers, and workers. By withdrawing investment funds from the public sector, or by recommending the release of government funds, the board helps to slow down or stimulate the economy. It may ask the government, for instance, to place military cloth orders at a slack time for the textile industry.

This description of the Labor Market Board illustrates how thoroughly the Swedes have organized their marriage of private enterprise and social welfare. Gosta Rehn, a Swedish trade union economist who developed the concept of the Labor Market Board, was asked to head the manpower division of the Organization for Economic Co-operation and Development (OECD) in Paris. This was a tribute by nineteen Western nations to the way Swedes had worked out a democratic allocation of labor.

Labor-management co-operation, which has given Sweden thirty years of industrial peace, is another intimate part of the nation's "middle way." Here, again, the Swedes have found the key to consensus between worker and employer. Collective bargaining on wages and working conditions is governed by two giant parent organizations—the Swedish Employers' Confederation (SAF), already mentioned, and the Confederation of Trade Unions (LO).

The latter, founded in 1898, embraces forty-three industrial unions, with more than one and a half million members. More than 90 per cent of Swedish industrial workers belong to LO. Employers are equally well organized. About 16,000 companies—industrial, handicrafts, transport, and others—belong to SAF, founded in 1902.

Periodically SAF and LO work out a framework agreement, defining the limits within which wage contracts should be concluded between individual employers and unions. This framework agreement is not binding on SAF and LO members. They are free to work out individual settlements. But since unions and employers jointly established the basic guidelines, pressure is heavy on members to conform.

The SAF concludes similar basic agreements with non-industrial unions—the Swedish Central Organization for

New and highly mechanized methods for drilling have been developed in the iron mines in Arctic Sweden.

Salaried Employees (TCO), grouping half a million white-collar workers, and the Confederation of Professional Associations (SACO), including lawyers, teachers, doctors, and other university graduates.

The Swedish Government stays strictly out of the picture, intervening only if elaborate arbitration machinery established by SAF and LO breaks down. A special Labor Court, including employer and union judges, settles disputes over interpretation of existing agreements.

Here is an important point. The Social Democratic Party, the government party, gets its major financing from

LO. Yet this union of workers agrees emphatically with employers that the government should stay out of collective bargaining. The SAF and LO made this clear in the basic agreement which established their collective bargaining partnership.

Disputes involving strikes and economic losses cannot always be avoided, the agreement states. Yet this does not "justify the replacement of the present freedom of collective bargaining" by state control. Neither should government force "upon Swedish employers and workers a regulation of working conditions."

This is a far cry from the system prevailing in Communist lands! There is no doubt that the Swedish system works. For the past fifteen years time lost due to strikes in Sweden averaged less than in nations like France and the United States.

For decades the Swedes have turned deliberately inward, to fashion the "middle way" for themselves. Their neutrality in two world wars typifies the course they have chosen. Swedes do involve themselves actively in humanitarian organizations like the Red Cross and peace forces of the United Nations in the Middle East and the Congo. But their aid programs to underdeveloped lands are relatively smaller than those of neighboring Norway, an active partner of NATO.

In power for more than thirty years, the Social Democratic Party now appears to be faltering at the polls. After years of growth the Social Democrats' share of votes began to dwindle in 1964, culminating in sharp losses in municipal elections in December 1966. Whoever wins the next elections, however, Sweden's blend of private enterprise and social welfare will prevail.

One can debate, as Swedes themselves do, whether Swedish young people, through their dress and habits, are protesting the lack of challenge in a social system which works with such sweet reasonableness. The answer, whatever it may be, does not undercut the contribution of Swedish Socialists. They showed the world how to protect citizens from birth to death, without destroying private ownership or democracy.

Great Britain, until the world-wide depression of the 1930's, had relatively little social legislation on its books. A rudimentary Poor Law Act, charging local authorities with care of the destitute, had been passed in England and Wales as early as 1601, and in Scotland in 1597. Before World War I, unemployment insurance to cover industrial workers had been created. Later other categories of workers were brought into the plan and compensation for injuries suffered on the job was added. Essentially, however, this comprised Britain's body of social legislation until after World War II, when the Labour Party came to power.

Stimulated in part by Franklin Roosevelt's New Deal across the Atlantic, Britain's wartime government in 1941 directed Sir William (later Lord) Beveridge to design a future program of British social services. This was a joint project of Conservatives, Liberals, and Labourites. The social welfare state which emerged in Britain, based on the Beveridge blueprint, was a collaborative effort, cutting across party lines.

None the less, Socialists gained primary credit for social legislation, for it was the Labour Party which British voters returned to power in 1945. Prime Minister Clement R. Attlee's new Labour regime added a distinctively Social-

Prime Minister Harold Wilson of Britain. He came into power when the Labour Party toppled the Conservatives in 1964.

ist touch by nationalizing coal mines, the railroads, and, briefly, the steel industry.

This sounds more Marxist than it really was. Clause four of the Labour Party constitution specifies that the means of production should be in workers' hands. In fact, however, influenced partly by Fabianism and greatly by the attitude of British trade unions, the Labour Party was moderate from the beginning. Reform of existing work laws, then the introduction of social welfare, were the party's chief goals.

Apart from steel, the industries which Labour nationalized were those that would have "gone bust," as one expert put it, if they had not been taken over. Railroads in capitalist France and West Germany are nationally owned, not on Socialist grounds, but simply because they lose more money than private industry can afford. Steel was a different question. As soon as the Tories (Conservatives) replaced Labour in 1951, they denationalized steel, holding fundamentally that Labour's takeover of this industry had been uneconomic.

Labour again is in power, having toppled the Conservatives in 1964. Once more the steel industry became a political football, involving emotions as well as economics. In March 1967 the government of Prime Minister Harold Wilson—with an eye to its left-wing Labourites—renationalized major steel companies, accounting for 90 per cent of Britain's iron and steel output. This about marks the limits of British nationalization, for, like Social Democrats on the Continent, Labour subscribes basically to private enterprise.

The party's great achievement was the enactment of social welfare. This was accomplished within a framework of four acts—the Family Allowances Act of 1945; the National Insurance Act of 1946; the National Insurance

Houses of Parliament in London overlook the Thames River.

(Industrial Injuries) Act of the same year; and the National Assistance Act of 1948. To these were added in 1948 the National Health Service, more popularly known, particularly by its critics, as "socialized medicine."

Beneath the umbrella of these acts and their amendments, the government administers a huge range of social services to virtually every subject of the Queen. A British mother, for example, gets £22 ($52.80) at the birth of each child. A family receives a weekly allowance for each child after the first.

Most men at sixty-five, and women at sixty, draw retirement pensions. Medical and hospital services are mostly free. A tourist who falls ill while visiting Britain receives free treatment. But a foreigner cannot enter Britain simply to get an operation without cost. There are checks against this.

British social security is based on the principle that benefits must be earned by contributions. A regularly employed Briton cannot choose whether or not to contribute to social security. The law says he must. This he does by going to his post office each week and buying a special stamp, which he affixes to his national insurance card, issued by the Ministry of Social Security. The citizen's weekly donation covers his participation in all parts of the social welfare system, including the National Health Service.

The latter, administered by the Ministry of Health, is by all odds the most expensive element in the whole structure of British social welfare. It is also the most controversial. Critics charge that "socialized medicine" encourages hypochondria, and hence waste.

British doctors are among the most vocal critics of the

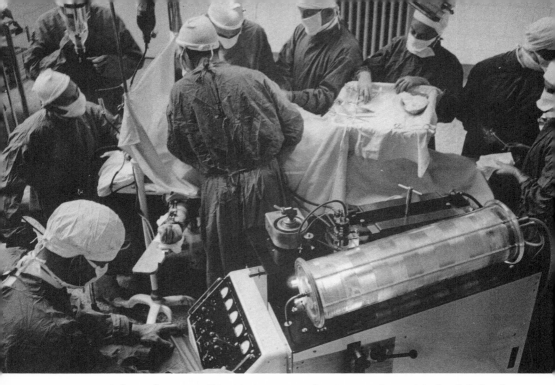

A *heart-lung machine is in use at the Postgraduate Medical School in Hammersmith, England.*

A *small girl has a tooth checked in the dental clinic at the Woodberry Down Health Center. Dental service is free to children.*

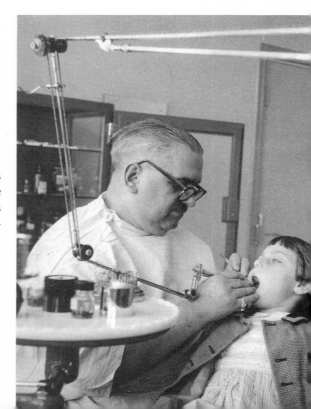

scheme. They claim to be overworked and underpaid, and say the situation is getting worse, not better. No doctor is forced to join the National Health Service. But most of them do, for few Britons care to pay for private medical treatment, when they can have it free.

A general practitioner (family doctor, or G.P., as the British call him), is allowed to have up to 3,500 National Health Service patients on his list. The average number is about 2,400. The doctor is paid a "capitation fee" for each patient. The doctor's base pay is his capitation fee, multiplied by the number of patients on his list.

This makes a high salary for a young G.P., whose income is likely to be above that of men starting out as lawyers or engineers. But the G.P. is virtually frozen at his starting level. If he begins with a large list, he cannot very much increase it. And their income is low, doctors assert, when divided into the number of hours they must work.

G.P.'s have another complaint. Medicine has become so specialized that often the family doctor simply diagnoses a case and hands his patient over to a specialist. The old comfortable relationship between family and doctor tends to disappear. "A capitation patient," grumbled one doctor, "regards the G.P. as he would a postman."

A rush of work nearly swamps doctors, clinics, and pharmacists. To prevent abuse of the system, the last Conservative government decreed a one shilling charge per prescription, which later was raised to two shillings. Bitterly opposed by Labour, this charge was abolished by Mr. Wilson's government.

Whatever administrative faults the system may have,

The old: A craftsman thatching the roof of the school in a small village in Somersetshire. Thatching roofs with straw is a craft of which few nowadays are master, and this school is believed to be the only one in England with a thatched roof.

the National Health Service has far more supporters than critics. Most working-class Britons are convinced the plan gives them a better medical deal than they had before. In the face of this, no future Tory prime minister is likely to tamper drastically with the National Health Service.

European social security systems, whether British, German, Swedish, or other, are essentially similar, though each government adds touches of its own. One thing the programs share in common is high cost. The economies of Britain, Sweden, and West Germany all are growing

The new: This shopping center in Harlow New Town, Essex, is characteristic of the new centers in many European cities.

less swiftly than the costs of administering social welfare. This produces a kind of two-edged consensus in Western Europe. Governments of whatever political hue support their social security programs. But they also grapple with how to hold these systems within bounds that taxpayers will support.

The postwar decades have seen many countries of Asia and Africa gain independence. The rulers of some of these lands label their economic policies "Socialist." Early in 1967, for instance, the government of Tanzania, a small East African republic, suddenly nationalized the country's large banks, trading corporations, and some manufacturing companies. This was based on the earlier example of

President Nasser, who had done the same in Egypt in the 1950's.

This type of "socialism" is not really Marxist, but rather an effort to wrest control of economies from former colonial hands. Morocco became independent in 1956. Yet for years French planters and industrialists continued to own and manage great segments of the kingdom's economy. Less patient than King Hassan of Morocco, other African rulers took private property away by fiat.

This is not socialism in the Western sense. India comes closer, through the social welfare policy of its Congress Party, which has governed the world's largest democracy— since India's first general elections in 1952. For mature social democracy, however, one looks primarily to Western Europe, where Marx and others planted the seeds.

The Italian, French, and other European Socialist parties have had complex histories of their own. By and large, however, their development falls within the pattern of the West German, Swedish, and British parties we have discussed. That pattern includes a minimum of nationalization, a good deal of social welfare, acceptance of the dominant role of private enterprise, and scrupulous regard for the democratic rights of the individual.

Capitalism
in Action

A COMMUNIST is a member of a political party. So is a
Socialist. But what is a capitalist? He may be a Democrat,
Republican, or belong to no party at all. If he lives in
Western Europe, he may vote for any one of a dozen
political parties. Capitalism, in other words, is an economic term, not a political party name. Communists and
Socialists also subscribe to economic theories, promoted
through parties created expressly for the purpose. But
capitalists have no single party.

Central figure in a capitalist society is the businessman.
He may own the corner drugstore, manage a textile factory, farm a thousand acres of corn, or be the banker
who supplies credit for new investment. Large or small,
this businessman shares one conviction with his fellows.
He cares passionately for private ownership. Homes, shops,
and factories—these should remain in private hands. But

beyond that, the whole body of productive resources—farm land, forests, coal, iron, and copper mines, telephone systems, railroads, air lines—should also be owned by individuals or groups of individuals, never by the state.

These resources, the businessman holds, should be turned into goods and services, earning profits for their owners. Such a system, Communists argue, exploits the workingman. The capitalist disagrees, for the seller cannot dictate who will buy his goods. He competes for the consumer's dollar and this competition, in the businessman's view, protects the public.

Goods of all sorts flow onto the market, seeking buyers. The law of supply and demand comes into operation, setting prices for shoes, raincoats, tennis racquets, cars, theater tickets, and canned fruit. If too many peaches are on grocers' shelves, prices will fall. If fruit growers pay a movie star to endorse peaches for radiant complexion, sales may jump—and so may prices.

The first man to open an automatic car wash in a neighborhood does a roaring business, so much so that the garage on the corner adds a car wash to its services. The garage owner charges $1.25, twenty-five cents less than the man down the street.

At first the garage has more business than it can handle. Then customers learn they don't get an inside vacuuming job for their $1.25. Some take their cars back to the more expensive shop. Others are content to save twenty-five cents and skip the vacuuming. The law of supply and demand has taken over.

Then a big car wash outfit from upstate moves into town, offering a wash *and* vacuuming for $1.25. This hits the smaller businessmen hard. The garage owner has his service station to fall back on, so he stays in business. But the first man, the pioneer, who taught the town to appreciate an automatic car wash, cannot lower his price and still break even. He has a brisk, tidy little business, so the upstate firm makes him a deal. It buys him out and he goes to work for the larger company.

Private ownership, free competition, banks to lend money—these are pillars of a capitalist society. Some businessmen win, others lose. But the consumer always wins, according to theory, because he forces the manufacturer to cater to his needs. Through clever advertising a businessman may create a market for a new line of goods, from hula hoops to contact lenses. Then he must offer value for money, for his competitors will jump on the bandwagon, adding wrinkles of their own.

Each reader may test this system for himself, by thinking for a moment of the supermarket, clothing store, and hardware shop where he and his family trade. Cast a mental eye over these merchants' well-stocked shelves. Who told them how much of what to buy? The mayor, city manager, or police chief? The answer, of course, is no one, except the consumer.

Multiply this experiment almost to infinity and one gets an idea of capitalism in action in the United States. The American economy is a gigantic, interlocking mesh of daily, hourly decisions taken by millions of men and women, acting independently of one another, motivated by their knowledge of the business conditions under which they work.

Supply and demand set a value on all goods and services offered. This value we call price. The price the consumer pays for a tape recorder or a pound of butter represents the most the consumer is willing to pay and the least the farmer or manufacturer can charge and still stay in business.

Wages, too, are a form of value. People set a higher value on doctors than on ministers. This must be so, or people would not willingly pay their doctors four or five times as much as they do their preachers. The doctor commands more in the market place than the lawyer, who earns more than the journalist, who gets more than a bricklayer, who commands more than a preacher. Values, or prices, fluctuate, according to the law of supply and demand.

The power of a pricing system was proven vividly in West Germany after World War II. Until 1948, the postwar German economy was stagnant. Gutted cities lay in ruins, few goods were being produced, and farmers refused to bring their crops to market. Instead they bartered food or sold it at excessive prices. I know men distinguished today in German life who grubbed in forests for nuts and berries to help feed their families.

People had money, but it was worthless. Three eggs or a loaf of bread had more value—and cost more—than an antique chair. Then, in May 1948, future Economics Minister Ludwig Erhard and other German officials introduced currency reform. They abolished the old Reichsmark and created a new currency unit, the Deutschemark.

Each man, woman, and child in West Germany was given an initial quota of 40 Deutschemarks. This meant that everyone in the country started out with the same amount of money. Later West Germans were allowed to convert their old Reichsmarks, up to a ceiling of 5,000, at the rate of 100 Reichsmarks to 6.5 Deutschemarks.

Essen, in the industrial Ruhr area of West Germany, has been almost completely rebuilt since World War II.

"Erhard's currency reform," remarked an American economist, "was brutal. But it worked."

Money again had value. No longer would shopping be a nightmare of barter, with the advantage going to the man who could pay one hundred dollars or a gold ring for a pound of meat. Hoarded goods began coming on the market, competing for sound money.

Dr. Erhard placed his currency reform in the context of a free-market economy. Government would keep its hands off the developing economic process. The law of supply and demand, Erhard reasoned, would stimulate

Former chancellor Ludwig Erhard introduced currency reforms in 1948 that boosted the postwar West German economy.

production, now that currency had become stable. He was right. The West German "miracle," as it was called, turned the Federal Republic into the free world's second largest industrial nation, after the United States.

The American businessman agrees with Dr. Erhard in wanting a minimum of government interference. Government is fine for collecting garbage, putting out fires, catching criminals, maintaining armed forces, and signing treaties. But the typical capitalist is strictly a private enterprise man. Here he differs from the Socialist, who favors government planning and some nationalization; and from the Communist, who advocates one-party control and almost total public ownership.

Carried to the limit, this capitalistic doctrine is known as laissez faire, literally "let (people) do (what they choose)." This doctrine was developed by Adam Smith in his book *Wealth of Nations,* published in 1776. Smith discovered that no central agency was controlling the operation of prices in a free-market economy. What was doing the work? Smith suggested an "Invisible Hand," impelling each individual businessman, while pursuing his own selfish ends, to contribute willy-nilly to the general good. Government interference would disrupt the free flow of competition, in Smith's view, and damage the economy.

This might be so, if perfect competition were the rule; if no single firm, by reason of its size and wealth, were able to influence the market in its favor. But businessmen, left on their own, do not tend toward perfect competition. Rather, like other human beings, they tend to gain as

Locomotive factory in Essen. After World War II, West Germany industry has developed rapidly, creating new highs in the economy.

much advantage for themselves as they can. The extension of this, in the past, led to the formation of trusts or cartels, in which giant firms conspired to divide up markets by prearrangement.

Company A would concentrate on certain lines of production, leaving Company B a clear field for other types of goods. Both would collaborate to see that no other firms entered the field. If necessary, A and B would cut their prices until small competitors were driven from the market. Once the field had been cleared of competition, up would go prices.

By the time Karl Marx wrote *Das Kapital* and *The Communist Manifesto*, the Industrial Revolution was in full swing, leading toward monopolistic capitalism of the type just described. Children of kindergarten age worked a full day in some European factories. Men went to work before dawn and stumbled home after dark. If a workman was injured on the job, there was no accident insurance to compensate him.

To Marx, Engels, and later Lenin, revolution promised the only way out for the workingman. The American people, through trial, error, sometimes bloodshed, and often good will, found another way, resulting in history's most spectacular organization of economic life. Before we discover how this was done, let us trace the roots of capitalism back through time.

Phoenician swimmers gathered murex shells for dye along the eastern Mediterranean shores of ancient Tyre, while their wives wove cloth at home. This cloth was dyed and sold to traders, who hired ships powered by sail and oar to carry the Tyrian purple across the sea to Egypt, Carthage, and Syracuse. Sometimes, needing money to finance their journeys, traders had recourse to the booths of money lenders in the narrow lanes of Tyre. This was capitalism in action, thousands of years ago.

Individuals were producing and selling goods for private profit, while other men provided ships, money, and labor for the goods to reach the market. Ever since those days, capitalism has been a constant, though changing, force in human history.

Feudalism, which dawned in Europe after the collapse of the western Roman Empire and that of Charlemagne, adapted capitalistic enterprise to its own special needs. Princes drew peasants, artisans, and tradesmen within the protective radius of moated walls, to grow food and make spears, armor, and household goods for the sprawling retinues of the feudal lord.

Craftsmen in the feudal age organized guilds, to guard the secrets of their work. Traders, journeying from town to fortified town, pooled their resources in trading companies and hired soldiers to protect caravans from marauding bands. River valleys, plains, and mountain passes became highways of trade. Growing cities along these trade routes progressively gained freedom to govern themselves, electing officials from their merchant class.

In 1241 the free north German cities of Lübeck and Hamburg signed a mutual defense agreement, which mushroomed into the Hanseatic League, an alliance of free mercantile cities along the North and Baltic seas. The beautiful old city of Bruges in Belgium still mirrors the wealth and splendor which Hanseatic merchants brought to the adornment of their palaces, guild halls, and homes. Even today Hamburg in West Germany calls itself the "Free and Hanseatic City of Hamburg."

Next came the rise of national states—France, England, Spain, the Netherlands, later Germany and Italy. National governments organized expeditions to conquer colonies for raw materials and as future markets. International trading companies, operating under the license and protection of governments at home, followed the flag to India, the East Indies, Africa.

Through all these developments labor still was powered by human muscle. Techniques of work remained largely as they had been hundreds of years before, based on the use of hand tools. Then, late in the eighteenth century, began the breakthrough to machinery. The inventor's skill was applied to the development of mechanical appliances, to be employed first in the textile industry, then in coal mining, iron smelting, and the making of steel. The invention of the steam engine by James Watt in 1769 provided a new source of power with which to drive machines.

Machinery could perform the work of many hands. But, to be effective, machines had to be grouped in factories. The concept of mass production was born, financed by businessmen who could buy machines and put them to work, earning more capital through the factory production of goods.

This development blossomed first in England, partly because a large merchant marine, backed up by the British navy, brought a never-ending stream of cotton, lumber, dyes, and other materials to an English homeland already rich in coal and iron. Industrialization spread to the United States in the first half of the nineteenth century, to France between 1820 and 1850, and to Germany much later, about 1870.

The introduction of machines enormously increased the wealth of nations. But this wealth had the unfortunate effect of dividing society into contending classes, for the newborn wealth flowed primarily to those few men who owned the means of production. The great masses of workers, whose hands alone no longer sufficed to earn a living, were plunged into the misery of long hours of factory labor. As industrial competition heightened, men, women, and children of the working class were driven to produce more. Theirs was the predicament of the captive Hebrews, whose Pharaoh decreed more bricks with less straw.

This was the capitalist world pictured by Marx. Governments of the day, he wrote, existed to enhance the bourgeoisie, at the expense of the proletariat. He over-

An air view of major industrial plants in Essen

stated, yet there was some truth in what he said. Only in 1833 had the British Parliament passed a law setting a minimum age on child labor in textile mills. That minimum was nine years!

One year later the British Government enunciated the principle of "less eligibility" for workhouses to which the poorest people were consigned. This meant that food and quarters must be inferior to those available to the most indigent person outside, lest idleness be encouraged. This typified the attitude of the comfortable—those who benefited most from the Industrial Revolution—that poverty somehow was linked to laziness.

Many people failed to appreciate that a poor and uneducated family might be overwhelmed by circumstances beyond its control. Until well into the twentieth century, courts, government, and public opinion in the United States and Europe came down on the side of business against labor.

The Industrial Revolution had set in motion forces of great benefit to mankind. Yet an unscrupulous few, if unchecked, could make life an ordeal for the many. How to apply those checks? Communism and socialism came into being with solutions of their own. Those who wanted to preserve the capitalist system, based on private ownership, had to come up with different answers.

The United States
Makes a Choice

BY NOW WE HAVE learned to be suspicious of labels that try to put nations into cut-and-dried categories. We have seen that Communist regimes are introducing profitability and the lending of investment funds at interest. Socialist governments, like those in Scandinavia and currently in Britain, turn out to favor private enterprise. Capitalist West Germany has a better social welfare program than most Communist countries.

We come now to a problem posed by the Industrial Revolution—how to control economic development to prevent boom and bust and how to put reins on too-ambitious businessmen. Communists tackled the problem by seizing power and imposing total government planning. That is one extreme. The other extreme is laissez-faire capitalism, which has now practically disappeared from the modern world.

Strung out between these two ends of the spectrum are those nations, Socialist and capitalist, which employ a "mixed economy." They believe in free enterprise and the right of the individual to dispose of his property as he sees fit. But circumstances required these societies to impose certain restraints on the individual's economic liberty.

If you own a small boat, and get into trouble off Cape Cod, the United States Coast Guard comes out to help you. The man who spied your plight from the tower on shore receives a salary. So do the men who pile into the motorized surfboat that churns out to save you. By the time you have been brought ashore, your afternoon outing has cost someone a lot of money. Do you foot the bill? You do not even tip the Coast Guard. The government pays the costs. This money the government gets from taxes.

Here, then, is a basic restraint on your economic liberty. You cannot spend all the money you earn. Some of it you and other citizens have to give to the government in the form of taxes. City governments charge a tax on your house and land. This tax helps to pay for policemen, firemen, and public schools. State governments collect excise, sales, and sometimes income taxes with which to build and maintain highways, recreation parks, prisons, hospitals, and state colleges. The army, its training, equipment, and deployment, is paid for through taxes. So is the Social Security check which comes to your grandfather's home every month. The federal government in Washington collects income and corporation taxes to make these services possible.

Taxes are an invasion on our privacy by government. But without taxes, we would lack the public services we all demand and which no citizen could buy for himself. All governments—Communist, Socialist, and capitalist—levy taxes.

The Bible, written by men who lived in hot and thirsty lands, describes the beauty of the cedars of Lebanon, casting shade, coolness, and providing wood for the Temple of Solomon. Today Lebanon has only two small groves of the majestic trees. Over the centuries Phoenicians, Romans, Turks, and other peoples heedlessly cut down the cedars for buildings and firewood. The Lebanese of today have been deprived of a priceless heritage which they cannot replace. If the United States adhered strictly to laissez faire, lumbermen could similarly level American forests. But they cannot do so, even if they wished, for laws exist to protect natural resources.

The United States Government requires car makers to include safety features in their automobiles. Factories must control smoke pouring from their chimneys and purify wastes before dumping them into rivers. Railroads, telephone systems, electrical power plants, and other public utilities are privately owned in the United States. But laws regulate the operation of these utilities. Banks and other financial institutions are regulated to protect depositors and investors. Your father puts his savings toward a college education for his children in a privately owned bank. Through poor management this bank could go out of business. But your father's savings are insured by the Federal Deposit Insurance Corporation, a government agency.

In September 1966 President Johnson signed a law raising minimum wages in the United States to $1.60 an hour, effective February 1968. This meant that even unskilled American workers were guaranteed at least this

President Lyndon B. Johnson presents a pen to Secretary of Labor
Willard Wirtz after signing minimum-wage bill at the White House.
In the background is George Meany, president of AFL-CIO.

much money to support their families. Other laws forbid
employers to discriminate on the grounds of race or color.
Negroes still are denied equal opportunity in many fields.
But without fair-employment laws, they would be worse
off than they are today.

We spoke of bigness as a potential danger arising from
the Industrial Revolution. The trend toward larger corporations still exists in the United States. The two hundred
largest companies in the nation account for more than

40 per cent of all goods and services produced. In 1958 their share of the market was 38 per cent, in 1947 only 30 per cent. By 1976, if the present trend continues, the two hundred largest firms will control more than half the nation's output.

The American economy is in the midst of a merger wave, the third in recent history. The Columbia Broadcasting System bought the New York Yankees. Newspapers invest in forests and paper mills. The Radio Corporation of America owns the Hertz car rental system. But these mergers no longer are uncontrolled, as they were in the nineteenth century. In 1890 the Sherman Antitrust Act outlawed restraint of trade through monopoly control or manipulation of markets and prices. Later laws expanded the scope of antitrust legislation.

Judges still must decide in each case whether bigness in itself is a crime, or whether—as in the CBS-New York Yankee merger—the combination does not restrain trade. As recently as 1961, executives of Westinghouse, General Electric, and other appliance firms, men highly respected in their communities, went to jail on conviction of conspiring to fix prices.

The nature of corporate bigness has changed from the heyday of laissez-faire capitalism. No longer, except in scattered cases, do individual families own giant companies. Ownership is vested in thousands of stockholders, each of whom owns a small share of the business. Management of the corporation is entrusted to salaried executives, theoretically responsible to stockholders, but in practice left largely on their own.

Bigness, of course, remains an enormous advantage, generating not only profits but research funds to plow

In a capitalist society, ownership in large corporations is vested in thousands of stockholders. At the annual stockholders' meeting of the Standard Oil Company

back into the development of better, more competitive, products. Thousands of small firms still go under, not as victims of restraint of trade, but simply because they cannot compete with giants.

All the various laws cited above, and there are many others, interfere with our liberty. But would we want to be without them? Suppose the United States Congress had passed no pure food and drug acts. Your mother might be uneasy every time she shopped, not knowing which canned goods were safe and which were not.

These laws were passed to cope with problems arising in industrialized societies incredibly more complex than societies ever had been before. Rules such as these regulate the conditions of trade, but do not prescribe who shall do what in the economy. The government, for ex-

186

(New Jersey), a stockholder, with portable microphone,
directs a question to the chairman, Michael L. Haider.
The president, J. Kenneth Jamieson, is at the right.

ample, forbade Bethlehem and Youngstown Steel to
merge, on antitrust grounds. But the government did not
go on to tell each company what steel products to make.
This would have been government planning.

Most Western societies, facing similar problems, developed bodies of regulatory laws, like those described
above. If we take three leading capitalist powers—the
United States, France, and West Germany, we find they
are roughly similar in two areas—in dealing out social
security and in placing limits on the freedom of individuals.

A third realm, however, is government planning. To
what extent shall government guide and control a nation's
economy? Communists do so totally. Socialists do so in a
modified way. The government in Sweden, for example,

187

through its Labor Market Board, high taxation, and control of national pension funds, dominates the Swedish capital market. This means the government, by releasing or withholding investment funds, can steer the economy.

France and West Germany are neighbors across the Rhine, each professing a capitalist system. In 1948 West Germany deliberately linked its currency reform to a free-market economy, in which market forces—the law of supply and demand—were allowed to operate without restrictions.

France, also facing the problem of postwar economic recovery, took another road. It instituted "the Plan." The direction of the French economy was to be determined by four-year development plans, drawn up by the government, working with representatives of business and labor. This system was considered essential for bringing the postwar French economy to its feet. With prosperity, however, economic goals changed and in February 1963 France added a new dimension to its planning.

Over a period of many years, a French official told me in Paris, the population of France had drifted steadily from west to east, following the lure of Paris and of industry. To illustrate this movement, the official slashed a line down through a wall map of France, from the Atlantic port of Le Havre to the Mediterranean port of Marseilles.

"East of that line," he declared, "is a concentration of industry, because of the coal and iron of the northeast and because of the transport hub of Paris. West of that line is a vast region comparatively drained of manpower, light in industry, far behind eastern France in economic development."

To correct this imbalance the French Government in 1963 launched a far-reaching program called "l'Aménagement du Territoire," or, roughly, efficient use of the resources of France. The goal was to reorient the development of France from a "sector" to a "regional" basis.

Hitherto each government ministry had prepared its annual budget in relative isolation from other ministries. One ministry would press the case for schools, another for housing, a third for modernization of farms. But there was no co-ordinating body to study the total needs of France and to suggest budgetary concentration on depressed regions.

This need was filled with the formation of the Aménagement du Territoire, responsible directly to the prime minister. "For example," an official of the department said, "suppose two new roads are under consideration—one a section of the thruway between Paris and Marseilles, the other a road connecting Brest and Rennes in Brittany.

"There is money enough for only one. Left to itself, the Ministry of Construction might decide on the Paris-Marseilles route, because of its heavy traffic pattern. Here the Aménagement du Territoire steps in, explains the pressing needs of backward Brittany, and assigns priority to the Brest-Rennes road. If the Ministry of Construction disagrees, the prime minister arbitrates and decides."

To prime the pump on projects such as this, this department of economic "brain trusters" has a multimillion dollar fund of its own, to be used at the prime minister's discretion.

"Three-fourths of the factories that will operate in France in thirty years," one planner declared, "do not exist today."

He rubbed his hands over the prospect, for he foresaw an opportunity to decentralize the industrial structure of the nation, pushing it south and west. To prod the movement along, the French Government is placing research and construction projects of its growing space industry in southwestern France.

Private industry can be persuaded to follow, it is realized, only if the government provides the transportation, marketing, and other facilities that will make provincial factories profitable. This is a gigantic enterprise, which will take years to accomplish.

French planners anticipate the need to invest heavily in developing about eight regional cities, to make them capable of becoming self-supporting centers. Each city thus selected would be considered the hub of an integrated regional complex, including roads, railroads, adequate schools and housing, and, where agriculture is concerned, regional marketing centers.

To aid the Aménagement du Territoire, France was divided into twenty-one administrative regions, each presided over by an official called a "co-ordinating prefect." Each such prefect, or chief administrator, became chairman of a "commission of regional economic development," comprising various economic specialists living in his region. Half of each commission is made up of representatives of labor, management, and farmers' organizations. The other half consists of elected officials, including town mayors and members of city councils.

All this is government planning with a vengeance, at least equal to that of Socialist Sweden and far ahead of Labour-governed Britain. Intervention by the French Government goes to extreme lengths in other ways. A French firm in financial difficulties, even if it goes bankrupt, cannot simply close its factory and discharge its workers. The final decision on the ailing company's future will be taken, not by management, but by the government.

The company first must notify the Ministry of Labor of its intention to shut down. A government work inspector—a highly qualified official, selected by competition—then is assigned to study the company's situation, including its financial records, its present and potential market, and the impact of that company's employment on the local community.

Following this exhaustive study, the work inspector issues his ruling. He may agree with the company's own decision. But he might also decree that the firm should continue its operation. In that case, and should management close down the factory anyway, the company's executives would be hauled into court and tried on charges of violating a state order. Fines and imprisonment could follow.

Ordinarily the process would not get this far. During the work inspector's study, the firm itself, government officials, both state and local, the Roman Catholic Church, and the trade unions involved would have been seeking some kind of compromise that would keep the plant running and save as many jobs as possible.

If, after all studies are completed, it is agreed by all parties concerned, including the unions, that part or all of the work force must indeed be laid off, the job layoff provisions of the French social security system come into play.

Discharged workers receive up to fifteen, eighteen, or even twenty months' severance pay from the firm, according to their category and length of service. Companies are required by law to hold in reserve sufficient funds to meet layoff contingencies. In addition, the discharged worker begins drawing unemployment benefits from the social security system, while all his other social welfare payments continue.

If the French Government's placement bureau finds a suitable new job for the discharged worker, requiring him to move, the state pays generous retraining and relocation benefits. Should the worker refuse to accept a job considered suitable, he would, however, lose all unemployment benefits.

This governmental power to intervene is designed to protect the workingman against sudden dislocation. French workers, on the other hand, are free to strike, provided their trade unions give advance notice. This freedom to strike is constitutionally protected in France. Unless the national interest is threatened, the government is reluctant to intervene. In March 1963, when President de Gaulle's government ordered striking coal miners back to work, Socialist, Communist, and Roman Catholic unions promptly called sympathy strikes to support the miners. Confronted by solid labor opposition, the government did not enforce its back-to-work order.

For a nation that expresses its individuality in so many ways and still professes capitalism, the degree of state planning in France might seem extraordinary. An explanation is gleaned from the wartime experience of the French people. Occupied in 1940 by the Germans, underground resistance became a unifying force among the French. People of many persuasions—including Communists—collaborated against the Germans. This resistance took place against the background of a deeply rooted social tradition in France, which over many decades prior to World War II had allowed conservative French farmers, the landed gentry, and the urban middle class to dominate French life at the expense of the working proletariat.

This tradition, already crumbling under the onslaught of Marxism, was decisively broken up by the experience of World War II, when the resistance drew loyal Frenchmen together. In 1944 the National Council of the Resistance called for something new in France—a complete system of social security to protect the worker and somewhat equalize the distribution of income in the country. This call was expanded and codified into law in 1945.

That is why the man on the motorbike, mentioned in the first chapter, doles out money monthly to French mothers from his leather pouch. That is how capitalist France came to have a social security system equivalent to that of West Germany or Sweden. The need to start afresh after the war explains also why individualistic Frenchmen accepted a degree of economic planning which Americans would reject.

In contrast to the French system, as the American economy grew in complexity and size, it came to be realized that the collective judgment of businessmen and consumers did not always add up to the general good. Cycles of boom and bust, prosperity and depression, cast uncertainty over millions of lives. Depressions, or "panics," had occurred with fair regularity throughout the first part of the current century, culminating in the 1929 stock market crash and the world-wide depression of the 1930's.

Meanwhile, the United States Government was growing to be the biggest business organization in the world, a

trend vastly accelerated by the enormous financial and
materiel demands levied by World War II. Today American commitments have become so large that the federal
government is scheduled to spend during fiscal year 1968
the staggering sum of $169,200,000,000, more than one-
fifth of the nation's gross national product. (Gross national
product, or GNP, is the value of a nation's total production
of goods and services. The American GNP in 1966 was
$740,000,000,000, a climb of $58,000,000,000 over the year
before.)

Expenditures of this magnitude—to pay for defense, the
debts of past wars, Social Security, highway programs,
federal aid to cities, to education, to the poor, and for a
host of other programs—vitally affect the operation of the
economy. Government had the duty, in the view of many

*Lunchtime in a Head Start class in East Harlem, New York City.
The special preschool program is being carried out in many poverty
areas.*

postwar American economists, to intervene to keep the economy from overheating or slowing down.

The essence of this postwar school of thought, called the "new economics," is as follows: if there is a shortage of demand, so that part of the nation's productive plant lies idle, the government should pump in new purchasing power. In March 1967, for example, as the economy appeared to be slowing, the White House released $791,-000,000 in federal funds for flood control, mortgage assistance, highway construction, and other projects. In short, the government created work.

The government also uses tax incentives as a fiscal tool to speed up business. Taxes may be so high that businessmen feel they have little money left over to invest in new plant and equipment. Their production stagnates. New

A VISTA antipoverty volunteer is greeted with pleasure by his Indian friends in Minnesota.

jobs are scarce. In this case the administration may ask Congress to lower taxes on investment funds, and to allow businessmen to write off depreciation of equipment more quickly. The cost of new machinery may be deducted from taxes, for example, in five years instead of ten. The effect of this is to leave more money in businessmen's hands for reinvestment.

Suppose the opposite condition prevails. Demand for goods has become so great that it outstrips supply. Prices rise, as businessmen compete for scarce labor and materials. These higher prices are passed on to the consumer and the cost of living climbs. The economy has become "overheated," or inflationary.

Here the government uses the tax tool in a different way. It asks Congress to raise taxes, thus draining purchasing power out of the economy. With less money available to be spent, demand slows down, comes into equilibrium with supply. Manipulation of taxes and the release of federal funds to create new work are called "fiscal" measures.

Also available are "monetary" devices, wielded by the Federal Reserve System of the United States. Created by Congress in 1913, the Federal Reserve System is an independent banking agency, charged with stabilizing the American economy. Most nations have a single central bank, located in the political capital of the country. Because the United States is so large in area, the Federal Reserve System has twelve regional banks, placed strategically throughout the country.

All private banks operating on a national scale are required to be members of the Federal Reserve System. Banks chartered by individual states can join voluntarily.

Member banks control more than 80 per cent of all deposits held by American banks.

The Federal Reserve System requires member banks to keep a certain percentage of their deposits as reserves, to pay off depositors who may wish to withdraw their funds. If a man deposits $1,000 in a member bank, $150 of this, let us say, must be deposited in a federal reserve bank as reserves. The remaining $850 is available to the bank to loan out at interest.

Perhaps, however, banks have loaned out so much credit that the economy is overheated. The Federal Reserve System reacts by increasing the reserve requirements of its member banks. A deposit of $1,000 now must be split,

The Federal Reserve building in Washington, D. C. There are twelve regional banks throughout the country.

perhaps, $200 to reserves and $800 available for loans. This Federal Reserve action, affecting thousands of banks, reduces the amount of money on the market.

The Federal Reserve System can further tighten up the capital market by raising its interest rate on loans to member banks. A bank borrowing one million dollars from the Federal Reserve System may be required to pay 5 per cent interest on this money, instead of 4½ per cent, as previously. This means the borrowing bank must raise the rate of interest it charges its own customers. In order to make money on its loans, the member bank now charges 5½ per cent, instead of its earlier 5 per cent rate. Fewer customers are willing to pay the higher interest. Credit is tighter, borrowing slows down.

To stimulate business activity, the Federal Reserve System does just the opposite. It lowers reserve requirements and/or lowers its interest rate to member banks. Governors of the Federal Reserve System operate independently of the executive branch of government, though banking officials and the United States Treasury are natural allies in trying to keep the economy in trim.

On the executive, or White House, side, a three-man Council of Economic Advisers was created, to advise the President on economic trends and suggest corrective remedies. No one claims the system works perfectly. But government economists point with pride to twenty years of nearly uninterrupted economic progress in the United States.

In recent years the government has experimented with a voluntary "guidelines" policy, to keep price and wage hikes in line with economic growth. Trade unions are urged to keep their wage demands within guidelines set by the White House. Big business likewise is pressed to keep prices stable. Neither side is obliged by law to obey. But Presidential pressure, in the form of a national spotlight on union and business affairs, can be intense.

We have seen how far the United States has moved from laissez-faire capitalism, in the realm of regulatory laws to protect the health and well-being of all citizens, and in the field of fiscal and monetary controls. There remains another area in which Americans long since have abandoned the rugged individualism of the past. That field is social welfare.

America's
House of Labor

In 1963 the Kaiser Steel Corporation and the United Steelworkers of America sealed a bargain designed to end strikes by giving workers a steadily growing stake in the company's progress. In the future more than eight thousand steelworkers at Kaiser's Fontana, California, factory would receive a share of whatever savings management could make by cutting production costs. As techniques for making steel improved, presumably these savings would grow.

Partly this would be done through automation. But workers were assured they would not lose their jobs thereby. Whatever served to cut costs would profit company and workers alike. Operation of the plan was to be supervised jointly by management and union officials.

Four years later the plan was working so well that the average Kaiser steelworker had received more than $2,000

Control panels for regulating the reducing mill at the Kaiser Steel plant in Fontana, California. The mill is used to reduce the gauge of steel before it is put through further processing.

in cash beyond his wages. Interviewed by Kimmis Hendrick of *The Christian Science Monitor*, company and union spokesmen spoke of the plan as "a unique step forward," reducing friction around the collective bargaining table.

Two generations earlier, American steelworkers had had a very different relationship with the men who hired them. In 1892 striking workers at the Carnegie steel plant at Homestead, Pennsylvania, fought an all-day gun battle with company police, in which seven men were killed. The immediate issue in the strike was a wage cut, imposed by management during an industry depression. But the wider struggle was over what role trade unions should play in American industrial life.

The Homestead strike was only one of many industrial disputes that erupted into violence during the turbulent decade of the 1890's, when militant trade unions clashed head-on with the owners of big business. American "proletariat and bourgeoisie" seemed as implacably opposed as any Karl Marx had written about in Europe. Few Americans in those troubled days could have foreseen that workers and company officials would sit down as amicably as happens today at Kaiser and numberless other plants in the United States.

Even in the darkest days of his oppression the American workingman, with relatively few exceptions, turned a deaf ear to the teachings of Marx. This fact, which did a good deal to shape the quality of American life, is all the more impressive when measured against the experience of Europe. There, the great Socialist and Communist parties based themselves on the working class and rose to prominence through the workingman's vote.

Critics of social welfare who dub the American program "creeping socialism" misuse the term, if they mean it politically. Social welfare in the United States, as elsewhere, certainly springs from concepts long advanced by Socialists. But the origin of American social security programs in no way was connected with a Socialist party, as was the case in Britain, Sweden, and other European countries.

Laborers in the United States ran up against the fundamental attachment of Americans to their private property. Indeed, the early American pioneers themselves were laboring men, farmers, and artisans. They cherished their homesteads, farms, and workshops which the work of their own hands had created. This concept of the sanctity of private property—that is, the self-interest of the individual —eventually merged with the concept of public interest. But most Americans accepted without question that the stability of their society rested on the right to hold, control, and dispose of property.

Further, the rigid class lines which had characterized European society were absent in the United States. Nothing barred a workingman of ability from climbing into the ranks of the middle class. The worker's dream was to advance his son beyond his own place in life. American executives boasted of their humble origins, something which seldom occurs in Europe.

The right of working people to vote came relatively early in the United States. So did the concept of free public education for all children, rich and poor. The American working class did not have to fight for these benefits. All these factors—reverence for private property, lack of class consciousness, equal political rights, free education—produced a social equilibrium in the United States, based on economic conservatism and dominated by the middle class.

Americans never minded a workingman struggling upward to own his own business. They admired him for it. But universally and violently the great American middle class reacted against any effort by labor to organize itself against propertied people. This seemed to Americans a basic threat to the American way of life. The result, until the New Deal of Franklin Roosevelt, was a coalition of government, courts, and public opinion against organized labor.

Socialism, much less communism, could not flourish in

such a climate. Wise labor leaders saw that unions could not afford to arouse the fear of Americans that their property rights were being threatened. Unions would only ruin themselves, by bringing into being restrictive anti-labor laws. Even today the word "Communist" arouses emotions among Americans which it does not do in France or Italy, where people are accustomed to the man next door voting for the Communist Party.

Against this background, many American trade unions, led by men like Samuel Gompers, a shrewd immigrant cigar maker, aimed primarily at economic goals—higher wages and shorter hours. Such goals did not strike at property rights and hence, Gompers reasoned, would not fundamentally alienate the middle class. As much as any other individual, Gompers—who had studied Marxism and found it inapplicable to the United States—shunted the American trade union movement away from communism and socialism.

The question then arose, How to achieve the working-man's economic goals? Hordes of immigrants were producing an overabundance of labor in the American market, much of it unskilled or semiskilled. In times of depression employers exploited this seemingly inexhaustible pool of cheap labor, refreshed by new streams of immigration from Europe. Labor, in such a situation, had little solidarity. Men were desperate for a job, any job.

The answer, to Gompers, lay in the formation of craft unions, composed of skilled workers united by a desire to protect their particular brand of skills. Carpenters, masons, his own cigar makers, hatters, printers, and cordwainers (shoemakers) should organize unions confined to their own crafts, excluding the unskilled. If the workers were

Samuel Gompers. Elected the first president of the AFL, he remained its leader almost forty years, until his death in 1924.

to win better working conditions from employers in a labor-flooded market, they could do this only by threatening to withhold needed skills from the market.

Craft unions, under Gompers' leadership, tried to build a fence around limited job opportunities to protect them for union members. This had to be done through collective bargaining. Employers had to be persuaded, by strikes, if necessary, to accept the craft union as its members' representative. Then the union had to stake out its right to "own" the jobs in a shop.

That is, if an employer were forced to let five men go, the union—not the front office—would decide which men should go. This decision was based on seniority. "Last hired, first fired," became the principle governing this aspect of collective bargaining. On wages, hours, and other working conditions, the union acted for all its members.

In times of prosperity, this system had the best chance

of working. In times of depression, when even skilled workers were overabundant, employers could and often did ignore the unions. Then union leaders strove simply to hold on to what gains they had made and bide their time, until the next cycle of opportunity rolled around.

The philosophy of craft unionism was summed up by Adolf Strasser, president of the International Cigar Makers' Union, appearing before the Senate Committee on Education and Labor in 1885, as pure and simple union-ism, aiming at practical, achievable goals within the exist-ing industrial system. "We have no ultimate ends," Strasser told the committee. "We are going on from day to day. We fight only for immediate objects—objects that can be realized in a few years."

Their goal was not the overthrow of government, or of private property, but simply the achievement of better working conditions for skilled American workers. In 1886 the representatives of twenty-five craft unions, totaling 150,000 members, organized the American Federation of Labor (AFL), better to promote their aims. Samuel Gompers was elected the first president of the AFL and, except for one year, he remained its leader until his death in 1924.

What about the great mass of unskilled and semiskilled workers, by far the majority of American laborers, who found no home in the AFL? Around them swirled much of the industrial turbulence of the mid- and late nineteenth century. Successive waves of immigration—as many as five million newcomers in a decade—coupled with the rapid introduction of machines following the Industrial Revolu-tion, depressed wages in a market crowded with men looking for jobs.

In the early 1850's two New York newspapers estimated eleven dollars weekly as the minimum needed by a workingman to sustain his family. Few factory workers were earning that much. Unskilled laborers in New York earned little more than one dollar per week for each person depending on them.

Gone were the days of paternalism, when some American mill and factory owners had practiced benevolence toward their workers. The latter decades of the century saw the rise of powerful business combinations, at that time unhampered by antitrust laws. Even craft workers suffered in this era, for machines and mass production reduced the bargaining power of their special skills.

Backed by the capital of wealthy men, including United States Government officials, the American Emigrant Company was formed to import workers of all kinds for America's burgeoning factories. This was the heyday of industrial barons, men who built empires in oil, steel, railroads, sugar, and other industries. Some of today's great foundations, established to promote human welfare, operate with capital amassed a century ago in the ruthless era of American laissez faire.

"Horizontal" unions, including only members of particular crafts, did not help the rank and file. They needed "vertical" unions, embracing all blue-collar employees in an industry, from floor sweepers up. This was the view of the Noble and Holy Order of the Knights of Labor, a mystical organization founded by nine tailors in Philadelphia in 1869.

Under the leadership of their second Grand Master Workman, Terence V. Powderly, the Knights of Labor set their sights on the total organization of American labor under one roof. Welcomed to membership in the Knights were all wage earners or former wage earners, except doctors, lawyers, bankers, gamblers, stockbrokers, and those who dealt in liquor.

Goals of the Knights included the eight-hour day, equal pay for men and women, abolition of child labor, the establishment of workers' co-operatives, and introduction of a graduated income tax. These goals were to be sought through education of the working class and arbitration with government and industry. Strikes were frowned upon by leaders of the Knights, though inevitably the sprawling loosely knit movement became involved in strikes, sometimes violent.

With 700,000 members in 1886, the Knights of Labor achieved a size and influence unique in American labor history to that date. But this very size conjured up in the public mind a vast shadowy threat to the established order. Powderly, a mild puritannical man, often overwhelmed by events beyond his control, was depicted as a labor czar, armed with power to bring the nation's business to a standstill.

In this atmosphere American industrial chiefs found ready public backing for their efforts to crush the Knights of Labor. The depression of 1873, when unemployed men had roamed city streets, sometimes rioting against their hopelessness; violence in the anthracite coal fields of Pennsylvania; the great Railway Strike of 1877, which had paralyzed much of the nation's traffic—these and other events had persuaded many Americans that the organization of labor was a first step toward revolution. During this bloody period, clashes between striking workers and police sometimes degenerated into pillaging and looting, in which tramps, hoodlums, and criminal elements took part.

To end the Railway Strike of 1877, President Hayes finally had called out federal troops. Public feeling had solidified against the striking railway workers. The latter, newspapers editorialized, might have legitimate grievances, but they had no right to throw other men out of work and jeopardize public property by going off the job.

This inflamed situation was roiled still more by a sprinkling of radical immigrants, preaching violent revolution and throwing bombs to make their point. The influence of these anarchists among labor itself was minimal. But the anarchists helped to poison the middle class against the workingman. Big business now girded to crush trade unions, and the Knights of Labor took the brunt. By the mid-1890's the chapter of American history written by the Noble and Holy Order of the Knights of Labor had ended.

It was during this period that Samuel Gompers fostered the concept of craft unionism, culminating in the formation of the AFL. For years afterward the American labor movement pursued a split course. Conservative "horizontal" unions of the American Federation of Labor worked toward immediate economic goals, while the great mass of industrial workers in factories, mines, and the railroads continued to battle for recognition from their employers.

A notable episode was the strike of the American Railway Union, organized and led by Eugene V. Debs, against the Pullman Palace Car Company in 1894. Like the great Railway Strike of 1877, the Pullman stoppage also halted train service nation-wide. This time railroad company executives found a new and devastating weapon to bring against the strikers. They asked for, and obtained, a federal court injunction, forbidding any person to interfere with interstate commerce and delivery of the mails. This meant that the strike was illegal.

In vain Debs appealed to Gompers of the AFL to call out labor across the country in support of the railway union. Gompers refused, holding—in line with craft-union thinking—that a general strike would only undercut labor gains already made.

The injunction ruling was challenged by the union all the way to the Supreme Court, which upheld the lower judgment. This crucial decision meant that the United States Government possessed inherent authority to prevent any obstruction to interstate commerce or to passage of the mails.

Again and again employers used this powerful weapon to break strikes. Ironically, injunctions sometimes were obtained under the Sherman Antitrust Act of 1890, on the grounds that unions were conspiring to restrict commerce. A law which had been designed to curb trusts was being turned by employers against their workers.

For their role in the Pullman strike, Debs and other union leaders went to jail. On his release the famous railway union founder turned to socialism. From 1900 until 1920, with the exception of 1916, Debs ran for President of the United States on a Socialist ticket. In 1912 the Socialist Party numbered its members at 118,000. Mayors in fifty-six American cities, and one thousand elected officials in cities and states, called themselves Socialists. This was the high-water mark of the American Socialist Party, which thereafter sank toward obscurity, collecting only twenty thousand votes in 1952. In 1960 the party stopped competing altogether.

Even when injunctions were used against his AFL, Gompers refused to listen to Socialist pleas for labor support. Socialists, he believed, were wrong, both economic-

Garment worker at her sewing machine. The abolition of sweat-shops was one of the early goals of the labor movement.

ally and politically. But Gompers did recognize the need to exert working-class influence at the polls, if unions were not to be hamstrung permanently by the government's injunction rule. "Reward your friends, punish your enemies," was the voting rule he urged on labor.

The accession of Theodore Roosevelt to the Presidency

in 1901, ushering in the "Progressive Era," paved the way for a more sympathetic public hearing of labor's needs. Roosevelt was a Republican. By and large, however, it was Democrats who responded more quickly than Republicans to the growing awareness of labor's political power.

In 1914, during the Democratic administration of Woodrow Wilson, Congress passed the Clayton Act, which outlawed—with certain loopholes—the use of injunctions in disputes between employers and employees. Big business still managed to fit its antistrike suits into loopholes of the new act, so that injunctions against unions did not completely cease. But at least they lessened. The Wilson years also saw legislation passed favoring American seamen and railroad workers. Finally, Congress in 1917 required a literacy test for immigrants, which began to dry up the wells of cheap labor which had undercut trade unionism in the United States.

A tide favorable to organized labor appeared to have set in. But this tide still brought benefits to only a small minority of American workers, for, prior to World War I, 90 per cent of all industrial labor in the United States remained unorganized. These largely unskilled workers had found the closed doors of AFL unions as hard to batter down as those of capitalist employers.

There ensued an ugly chapter in American labor history, when the militant Industrial Workers of the World, or "Wobblies," launched an attack against capitalism itself. Spearheaded by tough miners, harvest hands, and lumberjacks in the western United States, the Wobblies aimed at organizing downtrodden, migrant, and unskilled labor, as a first step toward overthrowing the capitalist system and establishing a government of workers.

The Wobblies never had a chance to achieve a goal so out of line with the thinking of most American workers, not to mention the middle class. By refusing to support the American war effort during World War I, and by striking key industries during the war, the IWW further outlawed itself from the mainstream of American life. Many of its members joined the postwar American Communist Party, and the Wobblies—one of whose key leaders fled to the Soviet Union—sank into insignificance as a union.[1]

At least this furious and radical group had pointed up the need for America's industrial workers to be responsibly organized in their own unions, if they were not to be used by people like the Wobblies. This need was muffled by the giddy prosperity of the "roaring twenties," in which labor also shared. Workers had unaccustomed money to spend, even began to dabble on the stock market. Drastic curbs on immigration during the 1920's strengthened labor's bargaining power.

None the less, the decade following the war saw big business generally dominant in the United States, with union membership falling away, partly because good times dulled a sense of urgency among many workers. Prosperity also revived the tendency of courts to grant antistrike injunctions, so that some labor leaders—despite fatter pay packets—felt their cause was losing ground.

---

[1] A series of Congressional acts, beginning in 1940 and culminating in 1954, effectively outlawed the Communist Party. The party was described as a subversive group, aiming at the forcible overthrow of the United States government. Since 1954 American Communists have led an organized but shadowy existence, barred from running candidates for public office.

This gave rise to America's first, brief, and only real labor party. In 1922 a group of farm, labor, and Socialist delegates founded the Conference for Progressive Political Action, whose platform called for public ownership of railroads and water power, as well as legislation to protect the workingman.

In 1924 this Progressive Party nominated Senator Robert M. La Follette of Wisconsin for President. Gompers, in a break with past policy, supported La Follette's candidacy, on the grounds that neither of the great political parties was heeding labor. Other AFL chieftains, including John L. Lewis of the United Mine Workers, threw their support to Republican candidate Calvin Coolidge. Still other labor spokesmen endorsed John W. Davis, the Democratic nominee. Coolidge won, La Follette collected less than five million votes, and the Progressive Party collapsed.

During this period of boom a number of employers hit upon a new scheme to weaken unions, called "welfare capitalism." Employers would make unions obsolete by giving their workers voluntarily all the benefits unions could demand.

Company cafeterias, clinics, and recreation facilities were set up. Group insurance policies were established, providing workers with cheap life insurance, so long as they stayed with the firm. Company retirement plans were born. Some employers made stock available to their workers. Others introduced profit-sharing plans. By 1926 more than four hundred such "company unions" had been established, with a total membership half as large as that of the AFL.

Benefits to workers under this welfare capitalism were

Labor leader John L. Lewis as he appeared in 1950 after successfully negotiating a new contract following a work stoppage of Pennsylvania mine workers.

real. But they were benefits dependent on employers' goodwill, and also on prosperity. Workers had little real say in the administration of company plans. Some of the most generous employers, as trade union leaders pointed out, were the most anti-union in their basic outlook.

In 1929 came the stock market crash, heralding the worst depression in the nation's history. By 1932 fifteen million men were out of work, shuffling in bread lines and soup kitchens, wandering the country in search of jobs. All Americans were hurt by the depression. Thousands of capitalists were wiped out. The middle class was deeply pinched. But, generally speaking, the blow fell hardest on industrial workers, whose jobs had disappeared and who had few resources on which to fall back. Welfare capitalism went by the boards, for employers had no money left for frills.

Even during the depths of this depression, labor scored one gain. Congress in 1932 passed the Norris-La Guardia Act, guaranteeing labor's right to organize and virtually outlawing antistrike injunctions.

The election of Franklin D. Roosevelt in 1932 marked a major step forward for American labor. No longer would courts and government combine to stack the deck against the workingman. Roosevelt perceived a basic need to ameliorate conflicts arising from the industrial age. This could be done only if both sides—management and labor—bargained from equal strength. Government from now on would see to it that labor had a friend in court, to preserve a balance in American industrial society.

Welfare in Modern Capitalism

STEP BY STEP, beginning with the various acts of President Roosevelt's New Deal, the United States eased into labor rights and, finally, social welfare. None of this was ideological, in a Marxist sense. American labor itself, in the first place, had rejected Marx and wanted nothing more than to secure its rights within a free enterprise system. Second, the New Deal was not a conscious attempt to socialize America, but an effort to pull the country out of depression and put men back to work.

Of supreme importance to workingmen was the 1935 National Labor Relations Act, or Wagner Act, named after the senator who had introduced it. This law gave workers the right to organize freely in unions, without interference from employers. The latter, moreover, were required by the act to bargain collectively over wages, hours, and other working conditions with employee representatives.

Workers elected the men who would represent them in collective bargaining. Delegates selected by a majority of workers would represent them all. This undercut company unions, which some employers still were using as a ploy against outside trade unions. A National Labor Relations Board (NLRB) was set up to administer the Wagner Act, with power to go to the courts to enforce collective bargaining rights.

The NLRB had no jurisdiction over the substance of the disputes that were being hammered out between employers and employees. It was not a mediation board. The NLRB acted solely to see that collective bargaining took place, as authorized by the Wagner Act. This was a tremendous step forward for labor and for the organized trade union movement.

A forerunner of the Wagner Act had been included in Roosevelt's National Industrial Recovery Act (NIRA) of 1933, which, however, the Supreme Court had declared unconstitutional in 1935. Anticipating the same result for the Wagner Act, industry fought against implementation of labor's new rights. Stool pigeons, labor spies, and strongarm squads of company police defended employer interests against labor "agitators." Some firms launched public relations campaigns to smear union leaders with a radical label. Unions fought back with the strike weapon. Then, in 1937, the Supreme Court upheld the Wagner Act, giving the NLRB full authority to enforce the law.

Meanwhile, an important development was unfolding within the ranks of labor itself. The old divergency between workers within the traditional crafts and mass production workers led, in 1935, to a breakaway of six unions from the AFL. Leading the breakaway was John L. Lewis, colorful, beetle-browed, forceful chief of American coal miners.

In 1938 the dissident unions formed the Congress of Industrial Organizations (CIO), pledged to unionize steel, automobile, and other industrial workers. First president of the CIO was John L. Lewis. Organized labor now wore two hats, a situation which lasted until 1955, when the AFL and CIO finally merged. Chosen as president of the combined labor giant was AFL president George Meany, a former plumber who still heads labor's united house.

By the time the merger took place the CIO not only had organized "Big Steel" and the automotive giants, but had expelled—after a series of union trials—eleven Communist-dominated member unions. American industrial workers were shown to be no more Marxist-inclined than

At a Labor-Management conference in 1945 were William Green (left), president of the AFL, and John L. Lewis (right).

Members of the New York Transit Workers Union listen to talks from union leaders near City Hall in New York during a transit strike in January 1966.

their craft brethren of the AFL. The CIO's demonstrated ability to clean its own house facilitated a merger of the two federations. The constitution of the combined AFL-CIO outlaws unions controlled by "Communists, Fascists, and other totalitarians."

Today AFL-CIO unions have a joint membership of nearly fifteen million men and women, including one million Canadian workers. Unions which reach across the frontier into Canada sometimes call themselves "international." About three million workers belong to unaffiliated

Teachers walk in a picket line outside of a Manhattan high school. With them is Albert Shanker, front center, head of the New York City United Federation of Teachers.

unions, most notably the giant International Brotherhood of Teamsters, which was expelled from the AFL-CIO on charges of corrupt leadership.

In 1935 Americans first tested the waters of social welfare. Congress that year passed the Social Security Act, designed to give elderly citizens a guaranteed monthly income. The plan was to be "actuarily sound," meaning an insurance scheme, administered by the government, whose costs would be covered by employer and employee contributions. Social Security is not charity, but constitutes a revolving trust fund, fed by the contributions of workers who one day will reap the benefits. None the less, the Social Security Act marked a far advance over the rugged individualism of the American past.

The 1937 Social Security payroll tax took one per cent of the first $3,000 of a worker's earnings, or a maximum of $30.

Inevitably, as living costs rose during World War II and after, Social Security payments were boosted time and again by Congress. The trend continues toward higher benefits and higher payroll contributions to meet the cost of the program.

But Social Security makes up only part of the vast social welfare package which Americans, like Europeans east and west of the Iron Curtain, have put together over the years. As Roosevelt's New Deal was succeeded by the New Frontier of President Kennedy and Mr. Johnson's Great Society, public opinion approved new categories of federal help to the poor.

In 1965, for example, Medicare—authorizing free hospital treatment and supplementary medical insurance for the aged—became law. This fell short of Britain's National Health Service, which gives free treatment to citizens of all ages. But the American program is growing. President Johnson wants Medicare broadened to cover one million disabled persons under sixty-five.

Congress made Medicare available to all Americans over sixty-five, whether or not they had paid Social Security taxes during their working years. This moved away from the philosophy that a person's benefits must be covered by his own contributions. Critics of Medicare, including many doctors, predicted that American hospitals would be inundated by elderly patients seeking free treat-

Many Americans who live in stricken areas such as this one in Gila River, Arizona, will be helped by the new War on Poverty.

ment. During the program's first year of operation—July 1, 1966, to June 30, 1967—about 15 per cent more elderly people entered hospitals than would have been the case without Medicare. Many of these people, however, were among those for whom the program was principally designed—senior Americans who could not afford medical treatment on their own.

Government officials now process 700,000 bills weekly from physicians with Medicare patients. The bulk of this spending is for hospital care, for which the federal government paid $2,400,000,000 during Medicare's first year. Smaller amounts were spent on patients treated outside hospitals. Medicare was costing more than had been estimated, admitted Robert M. Ball, Commissioner of Social Security. But the added cost, he maintained, still was being covered by the Social Security payroll tax. This meant that working Americans indirectly were paying the bills of those Medicare patients who had not contributed to Social Security themselves.

A growing shortage of doctors is of great concern in the United States. A conference sponsored by the Health, Education and Welfare Department of the United States Government in June 1967 concluded that demand for doctors' services will increase by at least one-third over the next ten years. The increase in number of physicians over the same period was estimated at 17 per cent. Medicare, it was pointed out, while not responsible for the shortage, contributed to it by boosting the demands being made on the nation's medical profession. These demands would greatly increase—including the administrative burden of processing bills through the government—if Medicare were extended to cover all citizens, as is the case in Britain and Sweden.

In his budget for the fiscal year ending June 30, 1968, Mr. Johnson proposed payments to the elderly and poor totaling $25,600,000,000, a rise of 16 per cent over the year before. This huge amount breaks down: cash payments, in cluding Social Security, $14,600,000,000; health, $4,200,-000,000; education and training, $3,800,000,000; economic and community development, including slum clearance projects and urban renewal, plus other services, $3,000,000,000.

Today relatively few Americans question the responsibility of government, through taxes, to aid the poor. But criticism is heard that the total program, having evolved haphazardly and been entrusted to many agencies, is wasteful and needs tightening up. This is exactly the criticism heard of social welfare programs in West Germany and other European lands. The sense of urgency is great, since American social welfare—despite its leapfrog growth —still leaves more than thirty million Americans, one-fifth of the population, below the poverty line.

Officials hold a person to be poor if his yearly income falls below $1,570, or that of a family of four under $3,200. Social Security payments to the aged do not benefit younger families. A new concept is in the air—guaranteed minimum income. Government should see to it that every family has enough income to bring it above the poverty line, thus technically abolishing poverty in the United States.

How to do it? Or whether to do it at all? This idea is as hotly debated today as Social Security was a generation ago. Critics assert that a sure monthly income would simply make the shiftless and lazy more so. The United States, proponents reply, is the only advanced industrial state without a family allowance system.

President Johnson has charged a commission of leading Americans to study the whole concept and report back to him by 1969. "The United States," the President declared, "is the first large nation in the history of the world wealthy enough to end poverty within its borders."

We have seen how the French Government delivers family allowances monthly to the door. Other Western nations have similar plans. Canada introduced family allowances in 1944. This is one solution being mulled over in the United States.

Another is called "negative income tax." A family whose

income falls below the poverty line would pay no income tax, but would receive back from the state a "negative tax" to help boost the family toward solvency.

A third idea is for the government to create what President Johnson called "residual public employment for all who lack private jobs." This would give unemployed people work in public parks, museums, libraries, hospitals, and other institutions. Does this sound familiar? It should, for this is what Sweden's Labor Market Board does, calling it "sheltered work."

Meanwhile, President Johnson's administration is striking at a root cause of poverty by trying to expand educational opportunities for the poor. An imaginative Head Start program sends helpers to work with preschool children, from four to six years old, in areas of acute poverty. The aim is to prepare these children to compete equally in school with youngsters from more privileged backgrounds.

Jennie M. Johnson, a teacher in Godfrey, Illinois, wrote enthusiastically about the Head Start program to *The Christian Science Monitor*:

> The first crop of Head Starters reached us this past year and there was simply no comparison to the advantages those children enjoyed. Our area is generally on a low level economically with a great many transients. Heretofore, the best I could hope for was about one-fifth of a class covering the optimum reading material. Nearly all of the '66–'67 children had Head Start and two-thirds covered the optimum of previous years plus much more. At the beginning of the year I was impressed with their ability to control and direct their attention.

Early in 1967 President Johnson asked Congress to ap-

Project Head Start. During the summer of 1965, more than 13,400 Child Development Centers were in operation.

prove an additional $135,000,000 for Head Start. He also proposed a "follow through" program, to carry Head Start into the first grades of school in poverty areas. The President also advocated the beginning of preschool training for slum-dwelling children three years old and younger.

To help prevent Head Start training from being wasted, the government in 1965 began to build a special Teacher Corps to serve in depressed area schools. This was designed to recruit teachers willing to work with children of the poor. Many established teachers in urban school systems tend to avoid schools in slum districts. This is understandable, but it also means that children who need the most help often get second-rate teaching.

By mid-1966 the Teacher Corps swung into action, staffed by eleven hundred volunteers, some of whom combined their classroom work with studies toward a master's degree. The program is too new for experts to evaluate its results. But Congress has assured the Teacher Corps funds through 1970.

Special programs of this type strengthened the Elementary and Secondary School Act of 1965, which provided federal funds for schools serving large numbers of children from low-income families. Included were millions of dollars yearly to enrich school libraries.

"We look toward the day when every child, no matter what his color or his family's means, gets the medical care he needs, starts school on an equal footing with his classmates, seeks as much education as he can absorb—in short, goes as far as his talents will take him."

These words might have belonged to a Communist or Socialist leader in Europe. In fact, they were spoken by President Johnson in 1967, when he submitted a twelve-point program to Congress on America's children and youth.

Housing is a third area of major concern to American welfare workers. Urban renewal, or the rehabilitation of slums in American cities, is one of the most urgent tasks facing the United States. Racial riots that have rocked American cities are bred in slums.

In four nights of rioting in Buffalo in June 1967, Negroes caused more than $150,000 of damage to homes and stores. Probing the background to the riots, investigators learned that 90,000 Negroes lived in a part of Buffalo where 60 per cent of the houses were substandard. Unemployment was high, schools were poor. Children in these schools scored far below the norm in reading skill. Lack

*President Johnson pens his signature to a $7,500,000,000 housing
bill. The bill contains a new rent-subsidy provision for the needy.*

of education, joblessness, and poor housing were found
to be linked. Buffalo is no exception; many American
cities harbor similar ghettos of discontent.

"In some of our urban areas," President Johnson told
Congress in 1966, "we must help rebuild entire sections
and neighborhoods containing, in some cases, as many
as 100,000 people. Working together, private enterprise
and Government must press forward with the task of providing homes and shops, parks and hospitals, and all the
other necessary parts of a flourishing community where
our people can come to live the good life. I will offer
other proposals to stimulate and reward planning for the
growth of entire metropolitan areas."

Mr. Johnson's use of the word "reward" was significant.

Urban renewal requires not only federal money but civic co-operation on the part of cities to be helped. Thus the government's urban renewal plans, part of the President's over-all attack on poverty, are carefully dovetailed with local efforts.

Cities with problems are invited to submit proposals for urban renovation to a federal government committee comprising four government departments—Labor, Housing and Urban Development, Health, Education and Welfare, and the Office of Economic Opportunity. By July 1967 this review committee had before it proposals from nearly two hundred American cities. The most needful will share in federal money appropriated by Congress for the Demonstration Cities Act of 1966, popularly called the "model cities" act. Other funds will follow. Municipal officials— mayors, town planners, social workers—will carry out the renewal projects themselves, backed up by federal money.

In St. Louis, Missouri, a private group of clergymen and businessmen received $68,000 in low-interest federal funds to rehabilitate dilapidated housing for the poor. This non-profit organization, called the Bicentennial Civic Improvement Corporation, will use the money to modernize eight rundown houses and sell them at low interest rates to deserving families. This was Bicentennial's second grant from Washington.

Two nonprofit corporations in New York City were given $7,000,000 by the Department of Labor to restore Brooklyn's Bedford-Stuyvesant Negro community, where nearly 370,000 people live. This restoration will include on-the-job training for residents, the creation of new job opportunities, renewal of slum housing, and construction of two health centers. Organized in December 1966 by

Senator Robert F. Kennedy, the corporations will draw on the talents of New York bankers, lawyers, and other business people.

The Negro as such is not singled out in the government's manifold social welfare activities. These are designed to help all the needy. Necessarily, however, many programs focus on the plight of American Negroes. Civil rights for all citizens are essential. But they must be buttressed by better education, from which, eventually, job opportunity should flow, and by better housing.

American workers had won their place in the sun, beginning with the New Deal. After World War II many influential Congressmen, spearheaded by Senator Robert A. Taft, held that the balance had been tipped too far and too fast in labor's favor. The Wagner Act, it was argued, had left the national interest dangerously exposed, by giving unions unrestricted freedom to strike.

The Taft-Hartley Law of 1947, passed over President Truman's veto, sought to redress the balance. The President of the United States, should he decide an impending strike was against the national interest, was authorized to order an eighty-day "cooling-off" period, during which workers could not walk off the job. Mr. Truman, despite his earlier veto, used this injunction ten times against unions. A later law, the Landrum-Griffin Act of 1959, empowered the government to probe union finances and internal affairs.

These laws, deeply resented by organized labor, attest to the continuing struggle which American unions and management still wage, with Congress refereeing on the sidelines. But today's contest is fought within a different framework than in pre-New Deal days. No one now questions labor's right to equality in the collective bargaining process. The effort is by men of good will on both sides—though they may vigorously disagree—to keep a balance struck.

When Americans were ready to give the workingman his due, they also were ready to accept social welfare. Labor rights and social security marched hand in hand in the United States. But not under a Socialist banner, for the American worker himself had rejected Karl Marx.

Computers and
the Future

A TALL, DOUR MAN stood alone, surrounded by moving gray ghosts of car bodies. He was the only human being in the vast shop. Toward him clanked an endless chain of welded metal shapes, each frame suspended from a giant hook. The man pulled a lever, a car frame dipped into a brimming vat, emerged dripping with gray paint, and clanked off.

This was the paint shop of a modern automobile plant in Germany. The man sensed our presence behind a glass partition, stared a moment, turned back to his work.

"He is always alone," said the official beside me quietly, "no one to talk to. He has asked for a raise to compensate."

We moved to the next stage of operations. Here another man was wedged into a glass cage, perched above two tanks of paint. Cars moved slowly toward him from the first man's shop, slowly disappeared into the vats, and came up brown. The man in the glass cage watched a control panel for warning signs. Like the first man, he, too, was alone in a great room, surrounded by moving shapes.

"Victims of automation," murmured the official. "I could not stand it, myself."

Already advanced industrial societies are being engulfed by automation and the computer age. The 1963 deal between the Kaiser Steel Corporation and its workers promised that no one would lose his job through automation. Packing houses, longshore firms in California, and other American companies have worked out similar arrangements. One method used is not to replace men who retire or leave the firm.

Consolidated Edison's steam electric turbine generator produces electric power for many customers. The one-million-kilowatt unit is the largest in the world.

But what about fresh waves of young men, coming onto the job market? They confront technological advances which, in the view of experts, will reduce available jobs in at least eighteen major American industries by 1970. Other expanding industries, including aerospace, electronics, and related fields, will create jobs that today do not exist. The problem, for unions and management alike, is to find ways to retrain people to do new kinds of work, without firing them from their old jobs in the process.

A commission appointed by President Kennedy came up with the following guidelines. First, technological progress could not and should not be stopped. But "this progress can and must be achieved without the sacrifice

Control console of the analog-digital computer enables this operator at Consolidated Edison to obtain within moments a variety of complex data.

of human values." Finally, the challenge was so great—comparable to a second Industrial Revolution—that government, industry, and unions would have to pool their efforts to meet it.

Automation is not confined to the United States. Socialist Sweden, capitalist West Germany, Labour-governed Britain—all are rationalizing their industries as fast as they can. But Western Europe faces a handicap vis-à-vis the United States, called the "technological gap."

At the beginning of 1967 sixty thousand computers were operating in the United States, four times as many as in all of Western Europe, including Britain. What does this mean? Simply that the United States, whose two hundred million people have a continent of riches to draw upon, is leaving its competitors behind.

A Swedish or German engineer may be able to design just as good a computer as an American. But the European does not work for a billion-dollar corporation able to leave him alone at his drawing board, test his successive models, and offer the finished product to a market of two hundred million persons, unhampered by national frontiers. Nor is any European company backed up by a government pouring billions of dollars yearly into defense and space research, in the form of contracts farmed out to private firms.

West Germany is the free world's second industrial power, edging ahead of Japan, Britain, and France. But when the West German looks across to the United States, this is what he sees: "In 1966," declared an official of the West German Ministry for Scientific Research, "the United States spent twenty-two billion dollars on scientific research and development. We Germans spent just over two billion dollars."

This workshop in Sweden for large electrical machines is among the most modern in the world. The illustration shows the boring of a rotor for a generator.

Put another way, West Germany devoted 1.6 per cent of its gross national product (GNP) to research and development. The United States spent 3 per cent of its GNP in the same field. By European standards, the Federal Republic did not do badly. France, Sweden, and Switzerland all spent about 1.6 per cent of GNP on research science. Only the United States and the Soviet Union among major powers soared to 3 per cent.

By 1970 West German officials hope to devote the same 3 per cent of gross national product to research as the United States now does. But, since the American GNP is seven times larger than that of West Germany, the gap in terms of resources poured in will continue to widen. This causes despair among many West Germans.

Other problems stand in the way. "In the United States," remarked a German professor, "seventy-two per cent of youngsters in any age group go on to secondary school. In West Germany eight per cent do this." He paused. "There lies one of the main reasons for the technological gap between our countries."

Nor does the Federal Republic hold its own, even among its comparatively few scientific graduates. Each year about 425 West German scientists emigrate. Most go to the United States. "Almost every good German scientist," commented an American diplomat, "has received at least one offer from an American university or firm—at twice to five times as much money as he can earn here."

Money is not the only lure. Research opportunity is equally important to young scientists, butting in vain against the traditional structure of West German universities. Unlike the departmental system in the United States, which allows researchers to share university laboratories and combine their efforts on projects, German universities are "pyramidal." A single professor controls a mathematics, physics, or other institute in a university, together with its laboratory, library, and funds. Younger teachers have access to these facilities only through the professor, which starves the research initiative of many young men.

Fifty per cent of German scientists interviewed in the United States said they would like to return home. The percentage of their wives holding this view was even higher. But the young scientists would not go back to German universities or research institutes—unless they were guaranteed funds and scope in which to work. At the Technische Hochschule in Munich and a few other institutions a start is being made in the introduction of teaching departments. But the path to reform is long.

West Germany is not unique in this respect. Details vary, but every Western European nation confronts a similar technological gap with the United States. On the one hand European talent flows to America. Britain alone lost four hundred aerospace technicians to the United States in 1966. On the other hand, European businessmen, eager to modernize their operations, find they must buy American computers and electronic equipment—if they want the latest and best.

The new Swedish "Sund" limber is push-button operated by one man from a separate cabin.

In this atomic reactor plant at Dounreay, Caithness, in northeastern Scotland, nuclear fuels are used to test materials and techniques, and to feed electricity into the national grid.

Many European firms buy patent and license rights to produce American-designed equipment and market it in Europe. This is not a one-way street. American manufacturers also reproduce Swedish, West German, and other machinery under license. But the traffic in this exchange overwhelmingly favors the United States.

European economists urge their politicians to get on with the job of unifying Europe. Only when national trade barriers fall, will Europe have the potential to match the United States. A good start has been made through the Common Market, embracing France, West Germany, Italy, Belgium, Holland, and Luxembourg. But this still leaves out the seven nations of the European Free Trade Association (EFTA), including two of Europe's most advanced countries, Britain and Sweden. Other EFTA members are Denmark, Norway, Austria, Switzerland, and Portugal. Five EFTA countries, led by Britain, plus other European states, currently are applying to join the Common Market.

From behind the Iron Curtain, the view is different. Communist governments would be delighted if they could only catch up with Western Europe, much less the United States. The industrial sophistication of Sweden or West Germany is a glittering goal, toward which Communist technocrats aspire. Except for Soviet scientists in aerospace and a few other fields, the Communists' technological gap lies west of the Iron Curtain, not across the Atlantic.

I recall an East German scientist, director of an advanced technical institute. "If only I could get my hands on a few western computers!" he exclaimed wistfully. "Only the Soviet Union makes computers in the Communist world."

Communists cannot politically afford to slip farther behind the West economically than they already are. This impels Communist leaders to deepen and broaden the economic reforms we have discussed. In March 1967 the Soviet Union began switching state farms to an incentive system. Hitherto only Soviet industry had been put on a profit and loss basis.

A recent U. S. Government report gave insight into the relative backwardness of the Soviet economy, which contrasts with the brilliant scientific advances of its space programs. At issue was whether the American Export-Import Bank should help Fiat finance a new automobile plant to be built in the Soviet Union.

The report pointed out that Soviet car production, currently about 210,000 cars per year, might be boosted by the new factory to a million units yearly in the early 1970's. This, it was said, would give the Soviets a stock of automobiles roughly equivalent to that of the United States in 1917. Currently the huge city of Moscow had a grand total of eight gas stations. The entire country had fewer than 2,000 service stations, against 211,000 in the United States.

However, in selected other fields the Soviets do well. An official Moscow press release stated that an American corporation had bought two 100-passenger Soviet hydrofoil ships, plus ten smaller hydrofoil craft, all to be delivered in 1967.

It is safe to forecast that, linked with the economic rivalry, the political struggle between the Communist and the free world systems will continue, with the great imponderable being the role of Communist China. Soviet leaders in the Kremlin are mature, in the sense that nuclear power—the ability to destroy the world at the touch of the button—has made them cautious. One can expect a wary contest for influence in the world between Washington and Moscow, short of a nuclear confrontation.

This may include some form of temporary alliance against a common Chinese threat. The outcome of such a league might strengthen, rather than weaken, the Soviet position in the world, if World War II was a precedent. Then, the invasion of Russia by German Fascists had forced Stalin to ally his country with the West. The joint defeat of Hitler brought about an extension of Communist power beyond the Soviet Union.

Fascism, particularly as practiced by Hitler, destroyed independent trade unions, Socialist and Communist parties, glorified war and nationalism, and boasted itself the representative of a master race. No parallel exists between European fascism and Chinese communism, except that both movements might impel the Soviets and Western allies uneasily toward each other.

That possibility belongs to the future and remains an open question. What does seem clear, however, fifty years after Lenin's Russian revolution, is that "capitalist" innovations behind the Iron Curtain, and welfare states and inventive social planning in the Western world, are changing the meaning of the terms communism, socialism, and capitalism. From three different starting points, these three politico-economic philosophies all appear to be drawing closer together, in practice at least, if not in theory.

Books for
Further Reading

Bernstein, Edouard, *Evolutionary Socialism,* trans. by Edith C. Harvey, 2nd ed. New York, Schocken Books, Inc., 1963.

Brown, J. F., *The New Eastern Europe, The Khruschshev Era and After.* New York, Frederick A. Praeger, Inc., 1966.

Buber, Martin, *Paths in Utopia.* Boston, Massachusetts, Beacon Press, 1958.

Chambre, Henri, *From Karl Marx to Mao Tse-Tung.* New York, P. J. Kenedy and Sons, 1963.

Cohen, Carl, ed., *Communism, Fascism, and Democracy.* New York, Random House, Inc., 1962.

Crossman, Richard, *The God that Failed.* New York, Bantam Books, Inc., 1960.

Djilas, Milovan, *The New Class.* New York, Frederick A. Praeger, Inc., 1957.

Dulles, Foster Rhea, *Labor in America: A History,* 3rd rev. ed. New York, Thomas Y. Crowell Company, 1966.

Galbraith, John K., *American Capitalism.* Boston, Massachusetts, Houghton Mifflin Company, 1956.

Hawthorne, Nathaniel, *Blithedale Romance.* New York, Doubleday and Company, Inc.

Herling, John, *Labor Unions in America.* Washington, D. C., Robert B. Luce, Inc., 1964.

Jackson, J. Hampden, *Marx, Proudhon and European Socialism.* New York, P. F. Collier, Inc., 1957.

Koestler, Arthur, *Darkness at Noon.* New York, Bantam Books, Inc., 1966.

Leonhard, Wolfgang, *Child of the Revolution.* London, William Collins, Sons and Co., Ltd., 1957.

Lovenstein, Meno, *Capitalism, Communism, Socialism.* New York, Scott, Foresman and Company, 1962.

Mao Tse-Tung, *Anthology of His Writings,* ed. by Anne Fremantle. New York, New American Library, 1962.

———, *Political Thought of Mao Tse-Tung,* trans. and ed. by Stuart Schram. New York, Frederick A. Praeger, Inc., 1963.

Marx, Karl, *Selected Writings in Sociology and Social Philosophy.* New York, McGraw-Hill Book Company, 1964.

———, and Engels, Friedrich, *The Communist Manifesto,* rev. ed. by J. Katz and F. B. Randall, trans. by S. Moore. New York, Washington Square Press, 1965.

Mendel, Arthur P., ed., *Essential Works of Marxism.* New York, Bantam Books, Inc., 1961.

Pasternak, Boris, *Doctor Zhivago.* New York, Pantheon Books, Inc., 1958.

Perlman, Selig, *A Theory of the Labor Movement.* New York, Augustus M. Kelley, 1949.

Rieber, Alfred J., and Nelson, Robert C., *A Study of the USSR and Communism: An Historical Approach.* New York, G. P. Putnam's Sons, 1964.

Rubinstein, Alvin Z., *Communist Political Systems.* Englewood Cliffs, New Jersey, Prentice-Hall, Inc., 1966.

Russell, Bertrand, *German Social Democracy.* New York, Simon and Schuster, Inc., 1965.

Samuelson, Paul A., *Economics: An Introductory Analysis,* 6th ed., New York, McGraw-Hill Book Company, 1964.

Schumpeter, Joseph A., *Capitalism, Socialism, and Democracy,* 3rd ed. New York, Harper and Brothers, 1950.

Smith, Adam, *Wealth of Nations.* New York, The Modern Library.

Solzhenitsyn, Alexander, *One Day in the Life of Ivan Denisovich.* New York, Frederick A. Praeger, Inc. 1963.

Index